A HOSPITAL VISITATION MANUAL

A Hospital Visitation Manual

Perry H. Biddle, Jr.

WILLIAM B. EERDMANS PUBLISHING COMPANY
GRAND RAPIDS, MICHIGAN / CAMBRIDGE, U.K.

First published 1988 by Abingdon Press, Nashville, Tennessee
© 1988 Abingdon Press

This updated and revised edition copyright © 1994 by
Wm. B. Eerdmans Publishing Co.
All rights reserved

Wm. B. Eerdmans Publishing Co.
2140 Oak Industrial Drive N.E., Grand Rapids, Michigan 49505 /
P.O. Box 163, Cambridge CB3 9PU U.K.
www.eerdmans.com

Printed in the United States of America

16 15 14 13 12 11   13 12 11 10 9 8

Library of Congress Cataloging-in-Publication Data

Biddle, Perry H., 1932-
Hospital visitation manual / Perry H. Biddle, Jr. — Updated and rev. ed.
p.   cm.
Rev. ed. of: Abingdon hospital visitation manual. © 1988.
Includes bibliographical references.
ISBN 978-0-8028-0698-7
1. Pastoral medicine — Handbooks, manuals, etc. 2. Church work with
the sick — Handbooks, manuals, etc. I. Biddle, Perry H., 1932-
Abingdon hospital visitation manual. II. Title.
BV4335.B48   1994
259′.4 — dc20   94-10496
                                        CIP

Unless otherwise noted, Scripture quotations are from the New Revised
Standard Version of the Bible, copyrighted © 1989 by the Division of Chris-
tian Education of the National Council of the Churches of Christ in the
U.S.A., and used by permission.

To the memory of my mother,
Daisy Yandell Biddle —
nurse, homemaker, mother —
who nurtured me in health and in the faith
with a touch of humor

OTHER PUBLICATIONS BY THE AUTHOR

A Funeral Manual (1994)
A Marriage Manual (1994)
Abingdon Funeral Manual (1976; revised 1984)
Abingdon Marriage Manual (1974; revised 1986)
Abingdon Hospital Visitation Manual (1988)
Humor and Healing (1994)
Lectionary Preaching Workbook, Year B (1987)
Lectionary Preaching Workbook, Year C (1988)
Marrying Again (1986)
Preaching the Lectionary, Year A (1989)
Preaching the Lectionary, Year B (1990)
Preaching the Lectionary, Year C (1991)
Reflections on Suicide (1992)
The Goodness of Marriage (1984)

CONTENTS

PREFACE

Angels fly because they take themselves lightly, someone has observed. Clergy and healthcare personnel need to learn to take themselves lightly while taking seriously their work with the sick. A sense of humor may be as valuable as a new medication in treating some illnesses. Or in conjunction with the medication, humor and a positive attitude can enable the patient to develop his or her own healing powers. I have described this relationship between humor and healing in my book *Humor and Healing* (see bibliography).

This book is written primarily for you, the working pastor, to enable you to become more effective in giving spiritual care to the sick both at home and in the hospital. You can make a difference in the recovery of patients as you encourage a positive attitude and a sense of humor. Pastors have resources of Scripture, prayer, empathy, and relationships to use as channels of God's healing power for the patient.

The first edition of this book was written a year before I was involved in a near-fatal auto wreck on August 24, 1989. This trauma resulted in fourteen weeks in the hospital and a recovery that is still ongoing four years later.

Friends jokingly wrote in get well notes that I didn't need to "field test" the hospital visitation manual!

The experience of being a patient is not one to wish on anyone, yet it gives one a different perspective on illness and recovery. I have been on both sides of the sickbed and definitely prefer the pastor's side, even though one of my physical therapists was a beauty queen!

The first four chapters of this manual will help you get acquainted with the hospital community and learn steps in visiting the sick. It also explains the pastor's role with the sick and the patient's relationship to the illness. Remember as you use this manual that the patient could easily be *you* and so follow Jesus' command to "Do unto others as you would have them do unto you." A split-second decision, a tiny virus, a sudden heart attack, or any number of traumas can put anyone into the hospital bed.

In recent years there has been intensive study of patients with specific illnesses to discover their emotional and physical reactions and spiritual needs. A number of these illnesses are discussed here, including AIDS. A suggested prayer and appropriate Scripture passages are listed for each illness, though the pastor is urged to develop other suitable prayers.

Limitations of space allow me only to suggest a few excellent resources on the specific needs of geriatric patients: Charles and Arline B. Peckham's *Thank You for Shaking My Hand* and *I Can Still Pray*, and Part IV, "Pastoral Care for the Aging," in *Pastor and Patient*, edited by Richard Dayringer (see bibliography).

Many people have made valuable suggestions for this book. I want to thank members of the Academy of Parish Clergy, Inc., who responded to my questionnaire at the 1987 Annual Convocation regarding their practices in pastoral care of the sick. I am indebted to parishioners who have ministered to me as I have attempted to give them pastoral care. Special thanks go to Blake and Jackie Brinkerhoff for sharing their insights and practices in caring for the spiritual needs of the sick. Many helpful insights were gained through informal discussions with a group of friends in Hendersonville, North Carolina.

In order for this book to be most useful, I also wanted input from "the other side" — from hospital staff. Martha Steel, a patient advocate, made suggestions, and Rev. Holly Nelson, chaplain at Vanderbilt University Hospital in Nashville, read the entire manuscript. I am grateful for their insights. Rev. Gary Brock, director of pastoral services at Vanderbilt Hospital, has been extremely helpful throughout the project, suggesting resources, reading the manuscript, and making useful comments.

Finally, I express my appreciation to my wife, Sue, the caring friend and soulmate who has encouraged and strengthened me throughout the years. She has been very supportive of this project; we have discussed it daily on our walks beside Old Hickory Lake.

Nashville, Tennessee   PERRY H. BIDDLE, JR.
September 1, 1993

PART I

PREPARING FOR PASTORAL CARE
FOR THE SICK

1

GETTING INTO THE HOSPITAL COMMUNITY

GETTING ORIENTED

One of the first tasks of new ministers in a community is to get acquainted with the hospitals that serve the members of their congregation.

A hospital is a unique community of people, much like a city. In fact, most hospitals have many features of a city, including power generating plants for emergencies, newspapers for employees, credit unions, laundry facilities, cleaning crews, governing bodies with administrators, communications systems with computer centers, and maintenance departments, in addition to the physicians, nursing staff, and patients.

If the hospital has a chaplain, the new minister should begin with a phone call to that office. Inquire about clergy parking and the location of the chaplain's office; ask to visit the chaplain in order to get acquainted with the hospital. If there is no chaplain, the office of patient services or social worker may provide some of these services.

In hospital ministry, you will sometimes be working closely with the chaplain, patient advocate, and social worker. Be sure to leave your business card with the chaplain's office or the information desk; they may be able to notify you when church members are admitted. Ask also to be put on the mailing list for continuing-education events for pastors sponsored by the hospital and chaplain's office. The chaplain or patient advocate can introduce you to the hospital community and point out the waiting rooms for various kinds of surgery, the emergency room (ER), the cafeteria (where pastors may visit with families), the chapel, the information center, and the file of patients by denomination.

It is also possible to become acquainted with the hospital by visiting it with another minister. There is an advantage to learning the ropes from someone who is already familiar with the hospital community and its policies. However, another minister may not be able to give you as thorough an introduction to the hospital as can the chaplain or other staff person.

THE MINISTER BELONGS!

When becoming oriented to the hospital community, the new minister should remember that, as a minister, you *belong* in the hospital. This is where a very important phase of the minister's work is done; many hours each week may be spent in hospital visitation. While the hospital may seem an alien world, the minister provides a vital part of the healing process to the patient and the health-care team.

It is important to learn the rules and governing policies of the hospital concerning the patients. The chaplain or patient advocate may supply a pamphlet with information about patients, hospital schedules, staff names, and so on. There also may be guidelines for ministers who visit. You will want to know the daily routine of mealtimes, bath time, and medical procedures, in order to avoid interrupting a patient's routine. In many hospitals ministers are encouraged to visit during normal visiting hours, which may run from 11:00 A.M. until 8:00 P.M. However, ministers usually are able to see patients in special need at other times, by first checking with the nurse's station for information and permission.

When the patient is in an intensive care unit (ICU) the pastor may be able to see the patient at times other than those set for family members. The pastor will need to check with the ICU nurse's station to get clearance to visit. Visits should usually be brief, five to seven minutes, according to the patient's condition. ICU nurses are becoming more willing for pastors to visit patients at odd times because of the positive effect of the visit on the patient. Humor, when appropriate, can help the patient deal with pain, self-pity, depression, boredom, and loneliness. Humor can also be a means of communicating with the patient that one cares. And humor can help the patient develop a more positive and hopeful attitude, which is very important in the healing process, as Bernie Siegel points out in his books (see bibliography).

Ministers may need to make calls late at night or before the doors are open in the morning, and you will need to know how to get into the hospital during those hours. In many hospitals one can enter through the emergency room, since it is open twenty-four hours a day, seven days a week.

Many hospitals provide identification badges to be worn when in the hospital. This can introduce the minister to hospital personnel and help prevent misunderstandings. A clerical collar or a cross also are positive identification of a minister's role and purpose for being in the hospital.

Security in hospitals is becoming more important for the protection of people and property, and ministers will need to recognize and accept the hospital policies. When making visits after hours, ministers, male or female, may want to call ahead to security and ask to be escorted into the hospital. Crime is more likely to occur in large parking lots when few people are around. Ask the chaplain's office about this on your initial visit.

THE SICK AT HOME

In addition to learning hospital rules, ministers will want to be sensitive to the unwritten rules of visiting sick persons in their homes. A telephone call will determine a convenient time to visit. As in the hospital, early morning hours often are taken up by baths, bed changing, or physical therapy. Late morning may be better than early afternoon, if the patient naps after lunch; middle to late afternoon may prove best. Sometimes the patient has had too many visitors or has just returned from tests or treatment, and the minister's visit would be more appreciated on another day.

As in the hospital, you should evaluate the situation and suit the call to the particular sick person's needs. If the person is cared for by a spouse, the visit may give the spouse an opportunity to run an errand or take some needed time alone.

Routine visits to shut-ins with long-term illnesses or handicaps can give both patient and family emotional support and spiritual guidance. Family members may be included in the visit, or you may help the patient indirectly by allowing a spouse or other family members to express their feelings privately. Friends of the patient also may receive emotional support from the minister.

While the rules governing visits to the sick at home are unwritten, ministers will want to be sensitive to each person's personal and family situation and respond appropriately.

THE ACUTELY OR CHRONICALLY ILL

There are two special categories of patients: the *acutely* ill, and the *chronically* ill. The acutely sick are those who will, with medical treatment and time, recover. The condition of the chronically ill will remain or gradually worsen over the years. Included among the acutely sick are the victims of accidents and others admitted to the emergency room. Many of the chronically ill will be in and out of hospitals over a period of years, and some of their care may be given temporarily in a nursing home. Both acutely and chronically ill patients need pastoral care that responds to their particular circumstances.

THE EMERGENCY ROOM

Ministers need to know where the emergency room entrance is located, since they may be called in the middle of the night to see an accident victim or someone with a sudden illness. It is important to identify yourself to the emergency room personnel as the *patient's minister* and then ask about visiting the patient.

You may need to wait while emergency medical procedures take place, and during this time you may be able to assist the family by making phone calls to other family members, employers, schools, or friends. Support for the family and friends may be the most important assistance a minister can offer in the emergency room. A calm, re-assuring approach will help family members deal with the emergency more effectively and also will be supportive for the patient.

A brief visit and prayer with the patient (whether apparently conscious or not) is almost always appropriate. You may be allowed only two or three minutes if treatment is being administered. Remember that a person who appears to be comatose may be able to hear and will appreciate a prayer and encouraging words. For that reason caution must be taken in what is said, since the patient may later recall everything.

A Scripture passage, prayer, and encouraging words to the comatose patient may be just the needed catalyst for healing. Humor, when it seems appropriate, can be used.

A minister who has received prior orientation to the hospital will be able to guide family members from the emergency waiting room to the chapel or prayer room, offices, telephones, cafeteria, and entrances and exits. You may need to go with a family member to admit the patient into the hospital and in other ways offer emotional support during the crisis. Often, just having another person along is calming for the patient's family.

If a patient dies in the emergency room, you may be able to help the family sort out the tasks that must be done — calling the funeral home, calling other family members, and making various arrangements. Again, a minister who remains calm in such a traumatic situation can best give guidance and emotional support.

When news of the death of the patient is given, you should ask the appropriate staff person if you and the family may come to the bedside of the deceased. If permission is granted, ask the family members if they would like to pray together at the bedside. You may want to invite any friends who are present and any members of the health-care team who are free to join hands with the family for prayer. The joining of hands can be very affirming as persons in distress feel physical assurance that they are not alone in facing a loss.

GETTING TO KNOW STAFF

In a small hospital, ministers may get to know the ER staff on a first-name basis, though in larger hospitals this is not likely to be possible. When ministers and hospital personnel know one another they can work more effectively as a team in dealing with emergencies. The ER staff may feel free to notify ministers when parishioners are brought in. Or they may ask for a minister's help with a patient from out of town or without a local minister. Often small hospitals depend on local clergy to serve as volunteer chaplains. Knowing the protocol involved and some or all of the personnel can be a valuable asset when a phone call asks a minister to meet a family whose daughter or son has been in an accident.

It is also good for the minister to meet the hospital administrator, director of nursing services, director of volunteers, and other people on the staff. Such personal contacts can be valuable when a minister needs help in cutting through red tape on behalf of a patient or needs some special information or assistance from hospital officials.

Getting to know the physicians depends somewhat upon the size of the community and the hospital. In a smaller hospital a minister is likely to know many of the physicians and will feel free to talk with them about a patient's medical condition and spiritual needs. In metropolitan areas this may not often occur, but even there physicians usually welcome a pastor's participation in the healing process. You may need to call the physician's office and ask that the physician return the call; do not be put off if the physician is not immediately available. In the hospital, you can write a note to the physician and ask that it be put on the patient's chart. This may be a request for a phone conversation or a time to meet with the physician and the patient's family.

There also may be an occasion to talk with a physician when you meet by chance in the hospital. But a minister and physician should be cautious not to appear to be talking behind the patient's back if you meet in or just outside a patient's room. A brief conversation together down the hall or in another room is much more desirable. A physician may, on occasion, call a minister regarding a parishioner patient's needs, but more often the minister will need to take the initiative.

The pastor should ask the chaplain if there is a patient advocate, ombudsman, or a hot line to the administrator that patients can use when needing special help in working through problems encountered in the hospital. Most hospitals have a "Patient's Rights" list that is helpful for patients. The pastor may on occasion need to assist the patient in contacting one of these resource persons. Or the pastor may help family members in contacting such resource persons on behalf of the patient. This is a more positive approach than playing the "Ain't it awful" game with patients.

Getting to know the nursing staff is another valuable aspect of becoming oriented to the hospital community. Ministers have much more direct contact with nurses than with other staff members when visiting patients. For this reason, you should get to know the nurses caring for a parishioner. Nurses may not be allowed to give as much information about a patient as the physician, but they can give some indication of the person's condition and whether the patient is available for a visit.

THE SMART PASTOR ALWAYS KNOCKS FIRST!

A good rule of thumb to follow in visiting patients is: *Check with the nurse's station first!* Tell the nurse on duty that you are a minister and name the person you would like to visit. The nurse either will tell you to go ahead or will check to see if the patient can see you. Many ministers would have saved themselves and the patient much embarrassment by *checking first.* This is true especially of a male minister visiting a female patient or a female visiting a male. Nurses appreciate the courtesy of a minister who follows the nurses' guidance in making hospital visits.

A second rule of thumb: *Always knock* before entering a hospital room. Call the patient's name, identify yourself, and ask if you may enter. Sometimes ministers familiar with a hospital will bypass the nurse's station and go directly to the patient's room. In such a case, *always* announce your presence by knocking or speaking to the patient *before fully opening the door.*

Pay attention to the signs on a patient's door. Notice if the light over the door is on; this indicates that a nurse is in the room. A minister should then check with the nurse's station to ask permission to visit the patient. Such precautions will make for a much more effective visit and much better relations with the nursing staff and the patient. You *belong* in the hospital, as a part of the team caring for the patient. But you should exercise the same courtesy in approaching a patient's room as you would in entering the patient's home.

2

THE HOSPITAL VISIT

DISCOVERING WHO IS SICK

The pastor has a number of ways of discovering when a parishioner is sick, either at home or in the hospital. An active "grapevine" of parishioners and friends can be one source. The hospital may notify you when a member has been admitted, or you may find a parishioner's name in the minister's file box at the information desk. The best way, of course, is to have a direct message from a patient-to-be, notifying the minister or the church when he or she is going into the hospital. Family and friends also should be encouraged to pass on this information.

No matter what you do, there still will be those who fail to let you know they are going into the hospital or are sick at home, and later complain that the pastor did not call. One seasoned pastor of a large church answers such complaints by asking, "How did your *doctor* know you were sick?" You may not want to be quite that blunt, but you should emphasize to the congregation each member's responsibility to notify you or the church office when someone becomes ill or goes to the hospital. Some patients become so turned in upon themselves that they forget to let the pastor know. Others, for various reasons, deliberately do not let the pastor know they are sick; they

13

may want privacy and do not wish to be visited, even by the pastor! Notices of someone being ill or going to the hospital should be written down in your notebook or calendar.

RESPONDING TO THE SICK PERSON

The nature of a patient's illness will determine whether to drop everything and go immediately to the hospital or wait until a time scheduled for visits. If the hospital is nearby you may choose to go immediately, but if a longer drive is involved, it is wise to call ahead to the nurse's station and ask if you can visit at the time you plan to arrive. If a patient can receive phone calls, you may choose to call the patient's room to arrange a convenient time to visit.

On routine visits, you might visit a patient on the front end of a series of hospital calls, then double back later if the patient is out of the room. After a period of time, a new pastor will get the "feel" of ways to avoid unnecessary trips or missing a visit because a patient has already gone home or is undergoing tests or treatment or an emergency operation.

ALTERNATIVES TO A PERSONAL VISIT

When the patient is not in the room, a message may be left at the nurse's station that you called and will be coming by another time. A brief note on a business card may be left by the patient's phone or with the nurse's station to be given to the patient. A written sentence of comforting Scripture and a brief prayer can be an effective substitute for a visit in person.

There are times when a minister cannot or *should not* visit in the hospital or with the sick at home. When you have a common cold you may feel guilty because it prevents calling on sick parishioners. But you may telephone, explain why a personal visit is not possible, and offer to pray with the patient by telephone. Or you may call the nurse's station and ask that the patient be notified of the phone message. Again, you may write a brief note to the sick person explaining why a visit cannot be made and add a sentence of Scripture and a brief prayer.

PROPER HAND WASHING

After arriving at the hospital and checking with the information desk to confirm a patient's room number (patients frequently are moved about as they progress toward health), you should go to a restroom and thoroughly wash your hands. The patient advocate in a large metropolitan hospital emphasizes the importance of "proper hand-washing techniques." This involves more than the usual washing with soap and water — it calls for *scrubbing* the hands thoroughly to flush away as many germs as possible. All who touch a patient should wash their hands before touching another patient in order to prevent spreading germs.

You should also wash your hands, again with the thorough scrubbing procedure, before *leaving* the hospital. You should not wash in front of a patient, however, for this could leave a confused or wrong message.

Avoiding Mixed Signals in Touching

Many pastors find that greeting a patient with a gentle handshake, placing a hand on the forehead, or holding a patient's hand for prayer can be very effective ways of comforting and assuring the person of loving care. So few people touch the patient unless they are doing some medical procedure that a gentle touch can be a welcome sign of caring.

The chaplain of a large teaching hospital cautions pastors and chaplains always to ask a child's permission to touch before extending a hand. This will give the child *control* over whether she or he is touched and will alert the child that this will be a friendly touch, not another painful injection or some other medical procedure. You also may want to ask adult patients if they would like to hold hands for a prayer together, or would like you to place a hand on the forehead during prayer.

A word of caution should be given at this point to the inexperienced pastor. Be aware that touching, kissing, embracing, or other physical contact can be misinterpreted by a patient as a sexual overture rather than as a caring expression of Christian love. While great assurance and comfort can be given by physical contact, make sure your contact with the patient or family members cannot be misconstrued.

Charles L. Rassieur has dealt with this issue as it relates to male pastors and female counselees in *The Problem Clergymen Don't Talk About* (Philadelphia: Westminster Press, 1976), available in seminary libraries.

AVOIDING OFFENSIVE ODORS AND SOUNDS

You also should be aware that patients are often supersensitive to odors. The odor of tobacco, after-shave lotion, or perfume can be offensive, even nauseating for some patients.

Speak in a normal voice, but more softly than usual, since the sick sometimes are more sensitive to loud sounds. A soothing, calming tone is preferred over a boisterous greeting.

ENTERING THE PATIENT'S ROOM

Either ask at the nurse's station whether a patient may be visited or knock on the door and ask permission to enter. When there is a "No Visitors" sign on the door, *always* ask at the nurse's station whether this applies to the pastor (usually it does not).

If special precautions are to be taken, such as wearing gloves, shoe covers, or a face mask, follow the nurse's instructions carefully. But disease is not the only reason for a "No Visitors" sign. The patient or physician may feel there have been too many visitors and the patient needs privacy.

When you enter a patient's room, you will naturally look at the patient's face. If there is a vision or hearing impairment, you should identify yourself. After an initial greeting, "listen with the eyes," as one professor of counseling tells students. A quick look around the room will reveal helpful clues for shaping the pastoral call. Who else is present? What is the patient's condition, as far as a quick first impression can determine — is the patient in bed, sitting in a chair, walking around? Are there few or many get-well cards, flowers, and gifts?

The patient's initial response, nonverbal as well as verbal, can give some clues to how the patient is feeling. Notice what medical equipment is being used and avoid disturbing it. A comment on cards and gifts can be a good opener as you remark on the love and care these gifts represent. If few or no cards can be seen, this may indicate few friends, and the patient may feel lonely.

The patient's needs and condition will determine whether to stand for the visit or be seated. A brief visit may seem more relaxed and longer if the minister sits. It is important to sit or stand so that patient and pastor can have easy eye contact and so that light from the window does not shine into the patient's eyes.

WHEN THE PATIENT IS ASLEEP

If a patient is asleep when you enter the room, there are several alternatives. (1) Go to the nurse's station and ask whether the patient can be awakened to see the pastor. (2) If a family member is present, ask if you should come back another time to visit. (3) If you are familiar with the patient's habit of catnapping during the day, quietly call the patient's name. *If* the patient is easily awakened, you may visit. (4) Leave a business card, a devotional pamphlet, or a written note. It is helpful for the patient to know the day and time the pastor called.

In the case of patients in a coma or so senile that they may not remember the pastor's call, a business card with a brief note can let the patient's family know when you called and how to reach you if needed.

Clearing the Way for a Visit

A patient may be watching television or listening to the radio when you enter the room. Many pastors ask whether the patient is watching a favorite television program or could the sound be turned down. Often the patient will say something like, "Oh, just turn it off. I just had it going and wasn't watching anything special." A more direct approach is to ask, "May I turn off the television for a few minutes while we visit?" Then offer to turn it back on when you leave, if the patient cannot operate the controls.

The purpose, of course, is to give your full attention to the patient and be able to hear and respond appropriately. Most patients welcome the pastor's visit and turn off the television. For some, however, a favorite program is the one constant event in their day or week and provides a relief from loneliness and boredom.

The Length of the Visit

The length of the visit will be determined by a patient's condition and need. A survey of ministers from a variety of denominations reveals that the average hospital visit is from five to fifteen minutes in length. None said less than five, and some indicate they visit from fifteen to twenty minutes.

A visit longer than twenty minutes may occasionally be warranted, but you must realize the strain such a visit puts on the patient. And the pastor's presence also puts a strain on members of the family who may be with the patient. The patient is not "up to strength," and it takes an effort to appear alert and cheerful.

Visiting with the Patient's Family

If you are visiting with a family in the waiting room during an operation, the same rule generally applies. While in some areas it is customary for the pastor to sit with the family for several hours, this can put a lot of stress on members of the family. They may feel they cannot take a nap, though they are exhausted. They may not visit with one another in a relaxed way when the minister is present.

Several short visits may be better than one long one, letting the family know where you can be reached by phone if needed. And you may check in with the family by phone as the operation progresses. This is a decision you will need to make based on expectations of the family, customs of the community, and what your time and work schedule will permit.

Of course, there are critical operations, such as surgery on a child, or brain or cancer surgery, during which the minister's presence may be wanted and needed for several hours. In such instances it may be wise to take a coffee break with a member of the family, or visit other patients, or go to the cafeteria for a meal. This allows the family to relax as well as giving yourself a break.

Guidelines for Visiting

You would do well to remember certain guidelines that apply to visiting with patients:

1. *Don't* lean on or sit on the bed. This will help avoid spreading infection and interfering with traction equipment or intravenous lines or wires that may not be visible.

It will also avoid pain for a patient who has recently undergone surgery.

2. *Don't* give the impression of prying into a patient's medical details. On the other hand, patients know their own illnesses as seen from the hospital bed, and this information can help shape the pastoral care needed. You may want to check later with family, nurses, or physicians about a patient's condition. The director of pastoral services of a large university hospital cautions pastors *not* to become a substitute physician, but advises that it may be important to know what is going on with a patient. And the patient is the primary source of this information.

3. *Do* offer to leave the room if medical personnel come in to perform some procedure. If a cleaning maintenance person comes in, you may say that you are the patient's minister and ask if the person could come back later. If a physician or nurse comes in, introduce yourself. In the case of a visit by the patient's physician, offer to leave the room and return later. In the case of a routine visit by a nurse, you may want to ask if the medical procedure could be done later in order not to interrupt the pastoral visit. Common sense and willingness to negotiate are advisable in such instances.

4. *Don't* argue or try to convince a patient of some issue. And don't get trapped into playing "Ain't it awful." The patient may complain about the awful food, the awful nursing care, the awful noise. A visit can be consumed by this game, which can be played with facial expressions and body language as well as with words. The patient may feel worse when you leave, from having dwelt on how awful things are, rather than dealing with positive feelings.

5. *Don't* be a bearer of bad news, such as information

about another patient who died of a similar illness. And don't contaminate a patient with a sad mood brought from a visit with another patient.

6. *Do* be natural.

7. *Do* be cheerful. "A cheerful heart is a good medicine, but a downcast spirit dries up the bones" (Prov. 17:22). Remember, the gospel is Good News!

Norman Cousins tells how humor helped him in a miraculous recovery and has related medical research on the positive effects of humor on the body/mind of patients. The pastor can help the patient cultivate a sense of humor and can supply humor resources (see bibliography).

8. *Do* offer to read Scripture and/or offer a prayer, if a patient wishes. If other patients are in a shared room, ask if they would like to be included in the prayer. The others may not have a minister, or their minister might not be available to visit.

9. *Don't* do all the talking. *Listen,* and be empathetic.

10. *Do* recognize that the topic a patient is *most* concerned about may not be mentioned until you have announced that you are leaving!

11. *Don't* assume that a comatose patient cannot hear. Hearing is the last sense to be lost, and many who recover can recall conversations that took place around them.

12. *Do,* when feasible, leave a recent church bulletin, prayer card, or inspirational pamphlet. (A page or two of Scripture or prayers from this manual may be photocopied for the patient.)

The "Real Concern" Phenomenon

A patient may bring up a real concern just as you announce that you are leaving. Chaplain Gary Brock, director of pastoral services at Vanderbilt University Hospital, explains that the person may have been testing the pastor-patient relationship to determine whether the "real" issue could be mentioned. Would the pastor understand? Could such a life-threatening matter even be discussed? The sensitive pastor will listen to the "real" issue and extend the visit as the situation may dictate.

In Chapter 4, "The Patient and Illness," suggestions are given for following up on the patient's understanding of the meaning of the illness and the theological issues involved. This last-minute raising of the "real" issue takes place as the patient gains courage, realizes it is "now or not during this visit," and finally blurts out what is really on his or her mind. Pastors who are conscious of this phenomenon will be able to follow up with a much more supportive ministry.

The Hospital Call as Informal Counseling

Howard Clinebell points out that ministers counsel within a church setting, in a network of relationships where many people already know one another. The pastor does see them in noncounseling settings, but many are seen also for informal counseling in the home or hospital. Some of these visits may be for spiritual nurture or pastoral care in general, but the visit becomes counseling when a person is aware of a problem and wants help. Clinebell describes the unique role of the pastor thus:

The professional role definition of ministers often allows them to take initiative in reaching out to those who need care and counseling. This is a unique and valuable professional advantage. . . . Pastoral calling is an expression of pastoral initiative, an important means of bringing a ministry of caring to people in their homes, and in so doing, identifying and building relationship bridges to those who need care and counseling.[1]

One way to enable persons to get the help they need is through the use of what Clinebell calls "openers." The judicious use of openers interrupts the superficial chit-chat of a social call and can move the visit to a deeper level, with a chance for meaningful dialogue between the pastor and the person in need. Openers will move the pastoral call to a discussion of issues that deal with values, relationships, and faith in God. A "question such as 'What seems to be the difficulty?' or 'Tell me a little about your situation?' usually opens the door for persons to describe their problems."[2] The minister may ask, "How are things going with you spiritually?" or make the observation, "I gather you have a burden on your mind." A question asked with empathy in a warm pastor-parishioner relationship can open an infected wound and allow it to drain. The minister should not shy away from taking such initiative.

Not every visit at home or in the hospital will result in conversation about significant problems. But the pastor

1. Howard Clinebell, *Basic Types of Pastoral Care and Counseling: Revised and Enlarged* (Nashville: Abingdon Press, 1984), p. 71.
2. Clinebell, pp. 73-74.

can help parishioners feel free to talk about their problems when they need to do so. We expect physicians to ask about our health and health habits. People should not be surprised when asked about their spiritual health by their pastor, their spiritual physician.

At the heart of counseling is the establishment of a relationship.

> Counseling consists of the establishment and subsequent utilization of a relationship; the quality of which can be described as *therapeutic* (healing), *maieutic* (facilitating birth and growth), and *reconciling* (restoring alienated relationships). This is the psychological environment where effective problem solving, healing, and growth can best occur. . . .
>
> A therapeutic relationship grows as the pastor pours herself or himself into being *with* the burdened person. This means concentrating on *listening*, and responding with caring empathy.[3]

The minister should encourage a sick parishioner to carry as much of his or her own burden as possible in order to avoid becoming dependent. Paul, writing to the Galatians, says, "Bear one another's burdens, and in this way you will fulfill the law of Christ" (6:2). But a few verses later he writes, "All must carry their own loads" (v. 5). A free paraphrase of these two verses is instructive for the pastor ministering to a patient, for it says in effect: "Help each other with your heavy trunks and so fulfill the law of Christ. But each person will have to carry his or her

3. Clinebell, pp. 74-75.

own suitcase." A problem may occur when a patient tries to carry a trunk of burdens all alone, and out of pride or a sense of independence refuses to accept or even admit a need for help. On the other hand, neurotic persons may "spill" their problems on the pastor, making their problems the pastor's problems. The pastor should then cope by listening with empathy.

The appropriate use of religious instruments, prayer, Scripture, and sacraments can enrich the pastoral visit to a sick person, says Clinebell:

> Because spiritual growth is the ultimate aim of pastoral care and counseling, ministers should use theological words, images, concepts, and stories, and the religious resources of prayer, Scripture, and sacraments with precision and care. Such symbols and practices mean many things to many people. For some they carry heavy, negative, emotional freight. They can be used in rigid, legalistic ways that arouse inappropriate guilt feelings and block creative dialogue and spiritual growth in counseling. . . .
>
> When religious resources are used appropriately they can be power-full instruments for nurturing spiritual wholeness, unique resources for pastoral care and counseling.[4]

One minister commented that he sometimes had failed to pray with a patient. Later, when he realized a prayer would have been appropriate, he regretted not having prayed. In a time of illness, a window to the soul may be

4. Clinebell, pp. 121-22.

open, and a person may hear God's word in a fresh and renewing way.

Kenneth Haugk describes what he calls "building a prayer" in a pastoral call: "Building a prayer simply means that you and the person discuss what needs to go into the prayer before you start to pray. . . . You discover the needs of the individual by asking open-ended questions, enabling the person to express his or her real concerns."[5] You may want to incorporate phrases from hymns and verses of Scripture in the prayer. And the patient may be asked to join in the Lord's Prayer. There are occasions when patients may wish to offer their own prayer, in addition to the pastor's. Portions of a hymn, poem, or Scripture passage may be selected for use as appropriate.

The minister should remember that confrontation is a greatly needed skill in pastoral counseling, though caution should be used with the sick, who may be unusually sensitive. "The central goal of confronting anyone is to enable *self-confrontation* — i.e., to help them face the behavior that hurts themselves and/or others and to feel guilt that therefore is appropriate."[6] Confrontation involves the use of the minister's authority, both as pastor and as ethical guide. But the use of this authority should be governed by love.

A QUANTUM CHANGE

People who are ill may have a life-changing experience as they suffer, confront their own death, and turn to God for

5. Kenneth Haugk, *Christian Caregiving: A Way of Life* (Minneapolis: Augsburg, 1984), p. 114.

6. Clinebell, p. 142.

help. Such changes are called quantum changes, conversions, or transformational changes. Professor William R. Miller of the University of New Mexico is a leading researcher on this subject. A person who undergoes a quantum change acquires a new outlook on life and a new set of values and personality traits. This often happens to people with addictions, such as alcoholics and drug addicts. (See bibliography for books on 12 Step Programs).

The pastor should be alert to signs that patients are struggling with deeper issues in their lives that may be a prelude to such a quantum change. Such changes are usually not sought or willed by the person. Rather, the change seems to be the work of an outside force, which for Christians is the Holy Spirit.

The result is a feeling of peace with the world and oneself. People often change when they sense a contradiction in their deepest held values. Or they may have an "Aha!" experience in which they perceive the facts of their lives differently. The pastor should be aware of this possibility and be a midwife to the birthing of the new person. The resources of the church, such as prayer, Scripture, and baptism, may help the person in making the rebirthing experience more meaningful. By empathetic listening the pastor can assist the transformed person in making sense of what has happened to her or him. This experience is not limited to those with addictions but may happen to an individual at any time in his or her life.

Catharsis in Counseling the Sick

A crucial part of nearly all counseling, in or out of the hospital, is what is called emotional catharsis, or emotional ventilation. Its purpose is to bring into the open the patient's thoughts and attitudes, along with the feelings and emotions associated with problems and conflicts. As the pastor provides an accepting counseling relationship in a safe environment, the patient is enabled to reveal burdensome feelings, explore them with the pastor, and find release. Clinebell outlines several approaches that tend to facilitate catharsis:

1. *Avoid asking informational questions* beyond those needed to obtain essential facts. Too many informational questions tend to pull the person away from feelings.

2. *Ask about feelings.* . . .

3. *Respond to feelings rather than just to the intellectual content.* Reflect feelings, using feeling words in doing so. . . .

4. *Watch for doors* that lead to the feeling level of communication. These include feeling words; emotion in the voice, face, or posture; protesting too much; self-contradictions (indicating inner conflicts); and discussion of need-satisfying relationships such as with parents, spouses, or children. . . .

5. *Be especially alert for negative feelings.* . . .

6. *Avoid premature interpretations* of why people function or feel certain ways and *premature advice.* Both of these are tempting traps since they offer the insecure counselor ways of feeling useful and in control, and thus less anxious. Both interpretations and advice tend to block the flow of feelings. It is important to be aware that after a session in which people pour out painful feelings and share intimate aspects of their

problems, they may feel embarrassment the next time they see the pastor.[7]

But the key to the patient's ability to find release lies in the pastor's ability to listen and respond to the patient's feelings.

What people learn from suffering and sickness when they have adequate spiritual guidance and support is shown in a study by William Goulooze, which consisted of more than two thousand responses to questionnaires. The purpose of the study was to discover how the experience of sickness, sorrow, or suffering had affected patients. The replies revealed a great amount of physical suffering — so great that it is almost beyond human comprehension. And accompanying the physical problems were mental problems, problems centered on rebellion against God and opposition to God's will — at least temporarily. Two spiritual questions were raised in connection with physical afflictions and mental illness: Why do humans suffer? Why am I afflicted? When illnesses were prolonged, the persons often became concerned with the problems of sinfulness and the need for personal self-examination. The pastor who is able to deal with *feelings* and does not short-circuit this process of self-examination, repentance, and acceptance of forgiveness will be giving pastoral care of the highest order.

Goulooze lists some of the lessons learned from illness that the study revealed, and these may be useful in making a hospital visit:

7. Clinebell, pp. 84-85.

1. God has a purpose in sending sickness and suffering to the individual. "I have felt from the beginning of my illness [seventeen years of arthritis] that God chose me for some purpose, and I can truthfully say I'm glad God chose me."

2. Jesus Christ cares for our needs and our burdens. "I was not alone; Jesus was with me all the way."

3. God answers the prayer of faith according to his divine will. "I have experienced that prayer changes everything."

4. Pain and suffering lead us closer to God.

5. Balanced faith in God's power to heal is rewarded with recovery. "When the doctors said I could not live, the Lord restored me."

6. God gives sufficient grace for every trial.

7. We can be sure of our salvation, the gift of God.

8. We can face death with confidence and calmness. "How completely the Lord Jesus Christ has taken the sting out of death."

9. The Bible is our great help in sickness and suffering. "There is power in God's Word. I am convinced of it."

10. The Holy Spirit is the constant companion of the Christian.

11. God gives us comfort for sorrow through his grace. "My greatest comfort is that I, with body and soul, belong to my faithful Savior Jesus Christ."

12. We can learn contentment through suffering. "Faith in the Lord has given us contentment in all our afflictions."

13. Thinking "health" is very important for our mental and spiritual well-being in the Lord. "Be

cheerful, always rejoicing in the Lord. Do not try to compare your illness with that of someone else. Do not groan when you suffer." "Waiting on the Lord is a technique that restores depleted energies." "As a blind person, I manage to find something to occupy my time. To me life is very interesting, more so than it is for a lot of sighted persons. I seldom think of my blindness, and the world, one might say, is at my fingertips. I have felt God's guidance and nearness throughout the years."

14. Cooperation with the doctors and the nurses is a necessity and a Christian's duty. "I shall have to place my faith in the doctors, trusting that the Lord has given them wisdom to know what is best for me."

15. God is our strength for every circumstance. "The Lord can help us the most when we cannot help ourselves." "God will supply all our needs."

16. "God gives his people songs in the night during suffering." "Not one night in all those seven years did I sleep well, but God gave me 'songs in the night'" (Job 35:10).

17. We can have fellowship in Christ's suffering. "Jesus himself suffered everything that can come to us; so he knows our weaknesses. He knows just how we need him and just what we need from him."[8]

In addition to these expressions of faith and growth through periods of illness and suffering, the persons responding indicated that some poems were helpful to them

8. William Goulooze, *Pastoral Psychology* (Grand Rapids: Baker Book House, 1950), pp. 73-76.

during their illness. The themes of the poems that gave courage and sustaining power are summarized in the following statements by Goulooze:

1. Frank recognition of afflictions, burdens, and trials.
2. The reality of death and the inner conflict to meet it.
3. God's sustaining grace in time of trial.
4. The sufficiency of Jesus Christ for every trial.
5. Peace of mind.
6. Complete surrender in the most trying circumstances.
7. Christ gives victory over sin, death, and the world.[9]

One poem stood out in popularity above all others — Annie Flint Johnson's hymn that begins "God has not promised skies always blue." (It can be found on page 167 of this book.)

These personal testimonies to the power of the Christian faith to sustain a person during illness underline the role of the pastor. Our challenge is to grow in effectiveness in making calls on the sick. "Some pastors, through personal experience, have been touched to a white heat in the fires of affliction," says Goulooze, "but others have failed to feel and understand the troubles of their flocks."[10] When the pastor comes to this phase of ministry with a deep sense of caring, dedicated to being used by God, calling on the sick will become more creative and effective.

9. Goulooze, p. 77.
10. Goulooze, p. 78.

3

THE ROLE OF THE PASTOR

Jesus Heals the Sick

In the parable of the Last Judgment, Jesus said, "I was sick, and you took care of me" (Matt. 25:36). The pastor's role in caring for the sick is part of the church's fulfillment of its mission to all who suffer. All Christians, laity and clergy, are called to visit the sick and minister to them. Jesus set the example of healing the sick and commanded the apostles and the seventy to heal:

> Jesus went throughout Galilee, teaching in their synagogues and proclaiming the good news of the kingdom and curing every disease and every sickness among the people. So his fame spread throughout all Syria, and they brought to him all the sick, those who were afflicted with various diseases and pains, demoniacs, epileptics, and paralytics, and he cured them. (Matt. 4:23-24)

When Jesus called his twelve disciples to him, he "gave them authority over unclean spirits, to cast them out, and to cure every disease and every sickness" (Matt. 10:1). Ministry to the sick is part of the ministry to which Christians are called in the name of Christ.

Lay Ministry to the Sick

This manual is designed particularly for the ordained minister's use. But it can also be used by laypeople, and one role of the pastor is to facilitate the ministry of the laity in caring for the sick. A complete description of ways to organize, equip, and motivate such a ministry is beyond the scope of this handbook, but a number of books and programs are available to assist in this very important task. Dr. Ken Haugk has developed a widely accepted and proven program for training, organizing, and supervising laypeople in caring for the sick and other persons with needs. For further information contact: Stephen Ministries, 1325 Boland, St. Louis, MO 63117; Tel. (314) 645-5511.

The lay members of most churches are already carrying out some kind of ministry to the sick. Programs such as that of the Stephen Ministries can enlarge and enhance this lay ministry by training that involves insights into ministering to the whole person, the role of prayer and the Bible, and other resources.

Visiting and Healing the Sick

Visiting and healing the sick has been a part of the church's traditional ministry for centuries. In the book of Acts we find Peter and John healing a man lame from birth. When the man asked for alms, Peter said, "I have no silver or gold, but what I have I give you; in the name of Jesus Christ of Nazareth, stand up and walk" (Acts 3:6). And Peter raised him to his feet, and the man walked and entered the temple, "leaping and praising God" (v. 8). Such compassionate caring for the sick set the church apart in the ancient world.

Jesus and the early church carried out this ministry because they understood that the very nature of God is compassionate mercy. The God of Israel did not forget the people suffering in slavery in Egypt, but led them out of exile. God and human beings are bound together in covenant, and God does not neglect the suffering.

We visit the sick because Christians live in covenant with God and with one another. We visit in order to break through the isolation caused by illness. Even as God took the initiative and came to us in Christ, so we take the initiative in going to those who are sick. Even as God reaches out to us in our isolation, we reach out to those confined to the sickroom. In calling on the sick as a representative of God's church and one of its caring members, the minister symbolizes the whole family of faith and the whole family of human beings.

All people need other people in order to sustain the will to live and the courage to combat illness. A minister's visit is a time of joining in the battle against illness, helping the patient cooperate with the health-care team in order to regain his or her health. In the process the minister often will give encouragement and emotional strength to deal with the pain and despair that often accompany illness.

PASTORAL CARE

One hospital chaplain has defined pastoral care as "the attempt to help others, through words, acts, and relationships, to experience as fully as possible the reality of God's presence and love in their lives."[1] The pastor, like the

1. Lawrence E. Holst, "The Hospital Chaplain: One Role, Many

hospital chaplain, fulfills this role in a variety of ways. Effective pastoral care results from both attitude and action. The major thrust is summed up in "seeking the best interest of another," but this attitude also results in concrete acts. While not having a corner on the market of caring for the spiritual needs of the sick, the pastor is looked to in a special way for spiritual guidance and support.

Some of the pastor's functions with the sick may consist more of loving acts than the proclamation of the good news. Through these loving acts, the minister communicates the presence of God. This presence is communicated through relationships and acts as well as through words.

Other more formal pastoral actions may be performed, in some cases exclusively by the pastor. These include the administration of the sacraments, prayer, reading and interpretation of Scripture, confession and absolution, and the leading of worship, including preaching. Through words, symbols, and actions, the pastor seeks to make explicit to the sick and to their families the presence and love of God.

INITIATING THE VISIT TO THE SICK

Visiting the sick and comforting the bereaved rank at the top of a pastor's duties and should be given priority. When a message is received that a parishioner has been in an accident and taken to the emergency room, the minister

---

Functions," in *Hospital Ministry: The Role of the Chaplain Today,* ed. Lawrence E. Holst (New York: Crossroad, 1985), p. 46.

must drop other tasks to respond to this emergency. The appropriate response may be to call the hospital to find out whether the person is there or has been transferred to another hospital and to discover the seriousness of the injury (if this information will be given), or to talk with a family member to see whether you are needed. A minor injury may not call for a minister's immediate presence, and a visit later in the patient's room would be more appropriate.

In addition to responding to calls for help, the minister must take the *initiative* in seeking out the sick. God's grace is the prime example of such initiative. The parable of the prodigal son illustrates the prior movement of God's love: The father in the story runs out to greet the prodigal while he is "yet far off." The sick person appreciates the minister's initiative in coming to visit rather than waiting to be asked.

The *initiating* decision is different from the *responding* decision, though both are valid and useful in the pastor's role. The visit to the sick person is almost always welcome and brings encouragement and hope. Daniel DeArment, a hospital chaplain, says, "People generally assume that we are not there to take, or to threaten, but to bring some message of *hope, faith, or love.* No other professional in the entire range of helping persons in our society has this kind of prerogative with people."[2] While the doctor, the psychiatrist, and the lawyer wait for the client to come, the pastor can and should take the initiative in *going to* people, especially the sick. Nurses go to patients usually

2. Daniel DeArment, "Initiative in Pastoral Relationships," in *Pastor and Patient,* ed. Richard Dayringer (New York: Jason Aronson, 1982), p. 11; italics added.

to carry out the doctor's instructions, but caring nurses know that patients appreciate a short visit or chat, or just a friendly Hello when a shift changes. The pastor's visit comes as a "gift," not as something requested.

Pastor to the Whole Person

A new appreciation of the relationship of mind and body in recent years has made the pastor's role with the sick even more important. Psychosomatic medicine has taught us the relationship of mind and body. The Hebrews understood humans to be unities — not spirits imprisoned in the body, as the Greeks believed. That unity of body, mind, and spirit becomes especially evident in times of illness. Psychotherapy (literally, "mind healing") seeks to reach further into the emotional roots of illness and health in order to enable those being treated to find release from fears that cripple and from deep-seated resentments (one of the most devastating emotions), so that they will be able to move into the future with greater freedom to achieve their potential. The role of the pastor in dealing with illness (which often has an underlying emotional or spiritual factor) should not be minimized. Mind and body are one interacting system. *Heal, whole, holy* — all three of these words are derived from the same linguistic root. The role of the pastor is thus even more central to the healing process, as the words, symbols, and actions of the *holy* are brought to bear on the sick in order that they may be *healed* and gain *wholeness*.

Pastor comes from the Latin word for *herdsman*. The role of pastor is that of shepherding the flock entrusted to the pastor's care. Christ said that he himself was the good shepherd who cares for the sheep. Scripture contrasts the good shepherd with the hireling who works for pay and is prone to run away when danger comes. The role of the pastor with the sick is to know the "sheep" in their setting, with their families and vocations and weaknesses. The pastor knows a sick person in a *systemic fashion,* rather than seeing an illness to be treated apart from family, work, and previous history. The value of seeing the person in this context cannot be overestimated. In both Old and New Testament writings, the *shepherd* is a key image for understanding God's caring love. For this reason the twenty-third psalm carries great meaning; the image of Christ as the Good Shepherd gives hope and comfort to those afflicted by illness. Pastors fulfill this role of caring for the flock by looking to Christ for guidance and strength.

THE PASTOR AS THEOLOGIAN

The pastor who makes calls on the sick is a *peripatetic theologian,* without the luxury of consulting a book on pastoral theology when a parishioner asks if God has sent this illness as punishment for past sins. The minister familiar with the issues raised by Job and others regarding the meaning of illness will be better prepared to reflect theologically with the patient.

The book of Job poses two major questions: Why do the righteous suffer? Why are the righteous pious? These questions call into doubt earlier explanations about God's works. Job's journey from security, health, and comfort to great suffering and loss, and his subsequent restoration, is a pattern a pastor may detect in patients in a lesser degree. At first Job responds to his losses with superficial trust and acceptance — a kind of denial stage, a very important defense mechanism for the human psyche. Then a crack opens in his composed emotional state. At first his wife tries to help. Then three friends come to console and comfort. The pastor should appreciate the fact that the friends sit with Job for seven days and nights without speaking a word to Job, "for they saw that his suffering was very great" (Job 2:13). This is instructive to the pastor, or to anyone who visits the sick or distressed: Silence and waiting with a listening ear may be more meaningful than speech.

Then Job speaks, cursing the day he was born (3:1). One of Job's friends responds with the common idea that "those who plow iniquity and sow trouble reap the same" (4:8). This notion of rewards and punishments carries over into the thinking of many as they wrestle with guilt and the feeling that God is punishing them by illness.

God speaks to Job, but only in the form of further questions, and the reader is drawn into the conversation as Job and God question each other. The problem is resolved in what might be termed a "covenanting convergence." The answer Job receives is not a rational explanation, but a meeting face-to-face with God in a sustaining relationship: "I had heard of you by the hearing of the ear, but now my eye sees you; therefore I despise myself, and repent in dust and ashes" (42:5-6).

A pastor would do well to reflect on the fact that while the human mind seeks to know the "why" of suffering, the answer of Scripture is the "who" that sustains the sufferer — God the Creator. Only when he comes face-to-face with God does Job come to himself. Thus knowledge of God and knowledge of self go hand in hand.

A new life is born as God creates a "new creature," the new Job. This is instructive: The patient you visit and who recovers from illness is a different person than he or she was before illness occurred. The person is either stronger in the faith, more trusting and hopeful, or less trusting, a more fearful and resentful individual. A pastor's role is to help the patient move *through* illness and become a stronger person. Ideally, the patient will become more insightful and more deeply committed to God in Christ. He or she will have experienced that God is truly our "refuge and strength" in time of trouble. And the pastor has been friend, shepherd, guide, theological teacher, and interpreter of Scripture.

THE PASTOR AND HEALTH-CARE ETHICS

The growing importance of the pastor's involvement in health-care ethics is pointed up by a recent essay by a leading pastor/ethicist who serves on ethics committees of several hospitals.

Healthcare Ethics and Clergy
by the Rev. Dr. Robert H. Crumby

The clinical setting is broadly defined as the place where the patient is observed and treated. This setting includes the hospital, rehabilitation center, nursing home and private residence. Unlike other professionals, clergy do not have to wait until the patient calls them, or contracts with them. Rather, they are expected to take the initiative in visiting and are expected to be present, especially, when notified of emergency situations.

Increasingly, physicians, nurses and other professional caregivers are becoming convinced of the therapeutic value of pastoral visits. They observe that prayer and a variety of spiritual resources impact positively on a patient's capacity to recover as well as to give significant comfort to patients and their families in the event of death or impending death. Calls to clergy by clinical staff persons are thus proliferating as the support of the spiritual caregiver is mixed with the medical and nursing treatment and as team decisions are facilitated.

Invitations by the physician/nurse teams are also increasing as the clergy assume important roles in the clinical decision making process. That widening process, impacted by technology and subsequent complex ethical dilemmas, has necessitated the change of designation from "medical ethics" to a more inclusive one, of "healthcare ethics." Such a change acknowledges that clinical decisions rightly begin and end with medical indications and subsequent medical procedures. They now include, however, additional considerations related to patient-family preferences, institutional concerns, legal and economic restraints, as well as religious and social values.

Clergy, therefore, are an integral part of clinical decision making activities because of the growing recognition that these religious and social values are extremely important facts in the search for truth at the bedside where *ethical* conclusions are appropriately determined. The Greek word *"ethikos"* and the Latin word *"moralis"* both mean "to decide" . . . to decide what is good rather than what is bad . . . to decide what is right as opposed to what is wrong. It is now being understood that one has not made a good medical decision unless that decision also encompasses legal, economic, *religious* and social values.

Since clergy are spending inordinate amounts of "out of office" time in clinical settings, it is natural that they are becoming a valuable resource as the decisions and procedures unfold and as they become part of the consensus building in a time of information sharing and ultimate group conclusion. It is imperative, therefore, that clergy as a profession seek to become knowledgeable in clinical ethical procedures and protocol, reasonably conversant with clinical terminology, somewhat comfortable and self-assured in clinical settings, and schooled in methodologies of clinical ethical decision making. A new day is dawning in healthcare, and clergy are going to have a critical involvement in the activities of that new day.[3]

Our Common Pilgrimage of Faith

Your effectiveness with the sick will depend not upon knowing the right answers or having a pleasing bedside

---

3. Unpublished essay, 1993, by Robert H. Crumby, Associate Director of the Center for Clinical and Research Ethics, Vanderbilt Medical Center, used with permission of the author. Dr. Crumby is a clinical ethicist at Donelson Hospital and at St. Thomas Hospital, Nashville, Tennessee. Additional guidance on health-care ethics can be found in *Troubled Voices: Stories of Illness and Ethics* by Richard M. Zaner (see bibliography).

manner, but rather upon *your own spiritual life*. Only as one dies to self and is raised to new life in Christ can one give of oneself as fully as possible to the person in need. Paul confessed what should be the goal of every pastor: "I have been crucified with Christ; and it is no longer I who live, but it is Christ who lives in me. And the life I now live in the flesh I live by faith in the Son of God, who loved me and gave himself for me" (Gal. 2:19-20).

None have attained perfection, but Paul says, "I press on to make [the resurrection from the dead] my own, because Christ Jesus has made me his own. . . . I press on toward the goal for the prize of the heavenly call of God in Christ Jesus" (Phil. 3:12, 14). Life in Christ is the source of strength, wisdom, and love for ministry to the sick, developed through lifelong prayer, meditation on Scripture, repentance, and acceptance of forgiveness.

The pastor comes to the bedside of the sick person as a fellow pilgrim on the journey of faith — to minister, but also to learn; to pray for and with the sick person, but also to be prayed for; to hear confession of sins, but also to confess; and together with the sick person, to claim God's grace in Jesus Christ which makes us whole.

4

THE PATIENT AND ILLNESS

THE PATIENT'S PERSPECTIVE

Someone has commented that every physician should experience major surgery and a period of recuperation lasting weeks and months. The same could be said of pastors! Both professionals undoubtedly would benefit from having "been there." It has been said that while surgery on someone else may be called minor, all surgery on oneself is major! Nothing can take the place of the hospital-bed view of illness, examination, and treatment or surgery.

A patient experiences illness from a perspective different from that of those who do not live with the illness twenty-four hours a day. Pastors are concerned with how patients see their illnesses and with the meaning the illnesses have for the patients. Some may have the positive attitude expressed by a woman who was forced by illness to lie on her back continuously. She said, "You can't help looking up when you are lying on your back!" Others may see their condition as that of a termite in a yo-yo, whirling around out of control while bouncing up and down, supported only by a thin string. You may need to help others search for the meaning of their illnesses. You might say something like this: "Often people who are sick wonder what their illness means for them. Do you?"

Many patients may shrug their shoulders and say, "I don't know. Guess it was just my time to get sick." But they usually say a great deal more, if you will listen. And the "more," says Robert B. Reeves, Jr., reveals that most do indeed read a message of some kind from their illness.[1]

The answer may come at different levels. This is where active listening is crucial. Rather than passing on to another subject — the weather, the food in the hospital, or a sports event — a time of silence may enable the patient to reflect more deeply. Reeves points out several levels of meaning the patient may find.

1. The first level is dissociation. The illness was something that just happened, and the patient feels no involvement. But if you listen, says Reeves, you may hear the patient tell you that "in some particular way he is not functioning properly. He may say such things as, 'I picked up a virus,' 'I slipped and fell,' 'I noticed a lump,' 'I was losing weight.'"[2] The sensitive pastor will pick up on this initial "first-person" hint that the patient does read a message from the illness that something is out of kilter — something that cannot be separated from the patient's own life.

2. A second level of meaning is an awareness of disharmony. The patient may say, "I've been going too hard" or "I've sort of fallen apart recently." "He conveys a sense of disaffection or alienation; a loss of meaning, direction, or

1. Robert B. Reeves, Jr., "Reading the Message of Illness," in *Pastor and Patient*, ed. Richard Dayringer (New York: Jason Aronson, 1982), p. 3.
2. Reeves, p. 4.

integrity; a bewildered groping for a selfhood that seems lost," says Reeves.[3] The patient's message is that his or her way of living is out of tune.

3. On a yet deeper level, the patient may feel responsible for the illness, that something he or she did or failed to do brought it on. While the patient may at first blame God, usually the finger of blame is turned from God to self, says Reeves. The patient may feel guilty for being unfaithful or dishonest or for hurting someone and now sees sickness as judgment deserved.

If you try to ease the patient's guilt by saying that this is not the way God deals with us, you may miss what the patient is saying beneath the spoken words. "For what the patient is saying . . . is that his *sickness is a consequence and expression of his way of life. It is his doing. He is responsible.* And that is a great deal more than to say it is a judgment for his sins."[4]

This feeling should always be explored since it may be unfounded or inappropriate. In that case, you can help the patient make this discovery. You can also help the patient sort out the exaggerations of guilt that are part of the regressions toward childhood which characterize every sick person, says Reeves.

GOING BEYOND GUILT

Regression by the patient reverts to the rewards and punishments meted out by parents. Some of the guilt involved in illness may be a rekindling of that earlier experience.

3. Reeves, p. 5.
4. Reeves, p. 6.

But you need to help the patient go beyond guilt to deal with the residue in self-accusation that *is* relevant, says Reeves — "evidence of desires, ambitions, deceptions, habits in which he was wittingly or unwittingly inviting trouble. It is necessary to get at these particulars, if the meaning of the message is to be understood and if the patient is to understand what his sickness has to say about his way of life."[5] If you fail to do this, the patient is left where he or she was *before* the illness.

While you are not to play physician, a pastor does teach values and can help people clarify their values and make changes in their life-style in order to move toward wholeness and health. A pastor can guide patients to explore what they are doing in their sicknesses, what pattern is being followed, and what hidden needs an illness is meeting. Reeves writes:

> For instance, what does his ulcer say about the way he habitually handles anger? When do the migraine headaches come, and what do they prevent — or save him from doing? The bad back, the arthritis, the cardiac arrhythmia, the spasms of emphysema — with what kinds of threat, danger, or crisis are they associated, and what do they accomplish? What alterations in style of life does this radical surgery imply, and which is the cart, which the horse?
>
> We need to be especially alert for possible connections between the form the patient's sickness takes and the state of his intimate relationships. Most sickness is in some degree a sign of a sick relationship, and the

5. Reeves, p. 7.

form of the sickness, or the organ that expresses it, may sometimes be a clue to what is wrong between the patient and those close to him.[6]

A pastor deals in faith, hope, love, forgiveness, and reconciliation, lack of which may have encouraged an illness and may hinder or prevent healing now or in the future.

You should be alert to persons who seem to have strong control over their conscious lives but who, for this very reason, are likely to suffer an illness that expresses basic relationships that are disrupted or broken. The body may express the distorted relationship in physical illness.

THE MESSAGE OF REEVALUATION

The final level in reading the message of illness, according to Reeves, is the message of *reevaluation*. If a patient has been able to move from guilty self-reproach to an understanding of a disease as an expression of the self, then the person is ready to accept the way values, goals, and life must be changed. Of course, the illness may have gone so far as to be irreversible, as in the case of advanced cancer. The person with a critical illness may be beyond physical healing, even with a change of heart and the best medical procedures. Even so, a change of heart changes the experience of the whole.

However, when the patient, pastor, and physician are able to catch the illness in time, the recovery, like recovery

6. Reeves, p. 7.

from alcohol or drug addiction, involves a turning from a former way of life to a new way of health and wholeness. This may come about through the deepest reading of the message of illness, says Reeves, an act by the patient that brings new understandings, relationships, sense of self, and a new life. For the Christian, this is a cooperation with the Spirit in making the person a "new creation" in Christ. But this must be the patient's own work, not something the pastor, family, or physician imposes. "The changed way of life must be an expression of himself. It must be his doing," asserts Reeves.[7] Since sickness is a crisis in selfhood, only when a person redefines his or her life-style does full recovery take place.

SUFFERING AND THEODICY

One question a patient in pain struggles with is this: Why does the power and goodness of God allow suffering in our lives and in the world? No pastor can avoid this question, which in theological terms is called *theodicy* — speaking justly of God amid the awesome fact of suffering. *Theodicy* comes from two words meaning *God* and *justice*. Thus it is concerned with seeking to justify or explain the goodness of God in relationship to the existence of evil. This may be the most difficult theological dimension of a pastor's work. A pastor may sit in the waiting room with a distraught father and mother as their child is dying in the critical care unit, and they ask, Why?

Thomas C. Oden suggests three sides to the "perplexing triangle" of any serious theodicy:

7. Reeves, p. 9.

God is unsurpassably good.
God is incomparably powerful.
Suffering and evil nonetheless exist. Why?

Oden cites three deficient solutions which must be rejected: "The first is the failure to look candidly at the reality of evil . . . pretending that evil does not have any psychological power or social resilience or durable reality." This is "the most frequent pastoral default in theodicy" and occurs when "out of good intention the pastor may so affirm the power and goodness of God as to look away from the throbbing pain or pretend that suffering has no power to demoralize. That does not aid the sufferer but, rather, intensifies the problem by avoidance."[8]

A second temptation is to give up the Christian affirmation of the insurmountable goodness of God. This may be done subtly as the pastor becomes demoralized by the wearing power of sin and, by manner if not by words, expresses the feeling that sin, evil, and suffering have an ultimacy which only God has.

A third temptation, says Oden, is to seek to "limit," as it were, God's power. The pastor or patient may admit that God tries hard in the face of evil and suffering, but is without final power to overcome them.[9]

The traditional Christian position has rejected all these solutions, but we cannot say nothing in the face of this question. We must speak from a biblical position, informed by the church's historical teaching.

---

8. Thomas C. Oden, *Pastoral Theology* (San Francisco: Harper & Row, 1983), p. 224.
9. Oden, p. 225.

Scripture teaches that God suffers with us (Heb. 2:9). As we struggle we are not alone, for God promises to be present with us in the midst of our suffering (2 Cor. 1:3-7). Not only will God be with us, but victory over temporal suffering in eternity is promised (Rom. 8:18). This victory is revealed in the suffering, death, and resurrection of Jesus Christ.

Oden lists a series of interrelated arguments or pastoral consolations from the Christian tradition, which together reflect in a powerful way on God's purpose and suffering.[10] Briefly summarized below, these arguments will not end suffering for the patient, but through the ages they have given insights for pastoral care.

1. The first consolation is that "God does not directly will suffering." While suffering may occur by divine permission as a result of finitude and sin, God created all things good, and his original wish for all humanity is unmitigated good.

2. "The free-will defense . . . can be a profound and practical consolation for suffering if we grasp it deeply enough." It is that God does not create evil; human freedom spawns the evils from which suffering emerges. The goodness that comes from finite freedom is greater than anything it is able to jeopardize. For God to have taken away freedom from humans would have eliminated intelligence and moral accountability.

3. God can draw good out of evil. The Judeo-Christian historical experience is that "God draws the greatest good out of the greatest disasters." Even when humans abuse freedom, God elicits good that otherwise could not have been elicited.

10. Oden, pp. 227-33.

4. "Evil does not limit God's power." Only the God of Scripture is powerful enough to risk living in communion and dialogue with "fallen, sinful, self-alienating creatures, and all this without threat to God's own identity or holiness!"[11] God does not simply stand by and watch history deteriorate, but continues to work to redeem the consequences of freedom abused.

5. The "lessons of affliction" may increase virtue — not because suffering is good, but because it is the means of a greater good: moral courage. People often grow through suffering.

The study of William Goulooze (referred to in Chapter 2) indicated that most persons had learned that God, in permitting suffering, had a purpose "they did not understand at first," but which in some way was revealed to them.[12] "They learned that God 'gives grace sufficient for every need,' that they could face death and suffering with calmness"; that Scripture at times was greatly comforting in ways not known before, "and that when they prayed from the heart 'Thy will be done,'" God did answer in the best way for them, even though an unexpected way. They also learned that faith enabled them "not to give in" to suffering, but to struggle for health and to be patient when their recovery was long and drawn out. They learned that through "entering the unwelcome sphere of suffering," they felt a deep bonding with suffering human beings everywhere, including the poor, the sick, and the hungry.[13]

11. Oden, p. 231.

12. See William Goulooze, *Pastoral Psychology* (Grand Rapids: Baker Book House, 1950), pp. 65ff.

13. Oden, pp. 232-33.

6. The power of suffering to cleanse and educate is a sixth consolation. Some people ask if their suffering is a chastisement. The book of Hebrews says, "For the Lord disciplines those whom he loves, and chastises every child whom he accepts" (12:6). Chastisement does not mean *to punish,* but *"to purify, cleanse,* or *make chaste."* Chastisement cleanses us; discipline teaches us. "God's purpose in suffering is not to increase pain," says Oden, "but rather to increase our capacity for joy by making out of pain something that would have been less good without it. . . . Jesus himself strongly repudiated the notion that material calamity is a punishment directly sent by God."[14]

7. A seventh consolation is that "individual suffering is socially rooted and socially redeemed": Each person suffers from the sins of others, and others from each individual's sin; and we all suffer for what our ancestors did or failed to do. We are not responsible for all that happens, but Oden points out that, while we may not understand all the mysteries of life, we can trust God's providential care in history, even in the face of overwhelming evil. "Trust in providence means precisely that: to rely on God's promise when all seems otherwise hopeless. Amid suffering that test is stiffened. From suffering something can be learned about providence that may not be accessible to learning in good times."[15]

8. "Suffering may put goodness in bolder relief," just as in a musical composition the unrestful chord increases the aesthetic enjoyment in the transition to a restful chord.

14. Oden, p. 233.

15. Oden, p. 234. See also Thomas Aquinas, *Summa Theologica,* 3 vols. (New York: Bensinger, 1947-48), vol. 1, p. 121.

"Sin-laden suffering is . . . like the meaningful dissonance" within providence. The mystery of suffering and evil has been compared to the two sides of an oriental rug. In this life we see only the back side of the rug, with its tied knots, loose threads, and the bare outline of a pattern. But in the age to come we shall see the front of the rug in all its beauty; we shall see the pattern God has been weaving in each of our lives.

This argument should be used with care, since "it may tend to ignore the harsh reality of suffering." It should be used sparingly and complemented with other forms of pastoral reasoning.

9. A ninth pastoral consolation focuses on "the values intrinsic to struggle." Change does not take place without pain, and "no growth occurs without struggle." Muscles must be pushed against a resistance in order to develop; without use, an arm or leg atrophies. Oden concludes that "perceived evils and suffering do not simply or necessarily corrupt and impede but, rather, form a significant part of our human education, permitted by God for a greater good — the nurturing of responsible free moral agency."[16]

10. A tenth consolation is "proportional receptivity of the good." God gives his complete goodness to us "in proportion to our capacity to receive it. Since we are finite . . . we are incapable of fully beholding or receiving God's goodness" in all its fullness and glory. "We can receive it

---

16. Oden, p. 238. See Nemesius of Emesa (late fourth century), *On the Matter of Man,* in *Cyril of Jerusalem and Nemesius of Emesa,* ed. William Telfer, Library of Christian Classics, vol. 4 (Philadelphia: Westminster Press, 1955).

only within the limits of our imperfection," moral dullness and limited vision.

11. "Evil as a privation of the good" is a pastoral consolation that perhaps has had greater influence than any other on Christian pastoral tradition. Augustine argued that "there is nothing to be called evil if there is nothing good." Evils are parasitic on the good; in themselves, evils "are not anything at all."[17]

From this we can see that even bereavement "depends wholly upon something good," the life and relationship "that has been lost. . . . No suffering exists except as it depends upon something that has being," says Oden, "and is in some sense good."

12. The twelfth and final consolation for the sick is the assertion that God, being good, would choose the world that "is best for the whole, even though some part may not participate as fully . . . in the good as some other part." Since the Scriptures teach that God is goodness personified and all-powerful, then in spite of the problems of this world, "because it is God's world [it] is the best possible world" for the fulfillment of God's purpose.[18]

Note that this is argued, not from experience, but "on the basis of the logic of God's goodness and power. The best of all possible worlds must be a world in which finite freedom exists rather than does not exist." When such freedom exists it is subject to abuse or else it would not

17. Oden, p. 239. See Augustine, *Enchiridion*, chap. 4, in *Augustine: Confessions and Enchiridion*, ed. A. C. Outler, Library of Christian Classics, vol. 7 (Philadelphia: Westminster Press, 1955), pp. 343-45.

18. Oden, p. 242.

be free, and everything that is free can go wrong — thus the possibility of evil, pain, and suffering.[19]

These twelve consolations must be used with caution. They are not easy answers to the problem of evil and suffering, but one or more may be of help when adapted to particular persons and their needs. Oden points out that "learning how to make this adaptation is a major part of the challenge of pastoral wisdom."[20]

A wise and skilled pastor may be able to help a patient to see, even in the midst of suffering, "how God draws good even out of evil," and that evil itself is, to some extent, "dependent upon good for its existence. But never should it be implied that the affliction is desirable in itself. . . . Affirm the creative possibilities within suffering," says Oden, "without becoming fixated on the value of suffering itself."[21] The problem of evil and suffering can never be solved, but the hope of resurrection is that God will set right what is fallen, and evil will be judged and overcome in the end. This is our greatest consolation in this life and in the life to come.

The critical role of the pastor and the church community in providing pastoral care for the patient is emphasized by recent research from many disciplines. This research indicates that the immune system, which enables the body to combat infectious diseases, is modulated in crucial ways by messages from the brain, many of which are produced by the emotions associated with tension and stress. And the brain is influenced by signals from the immune system.

19. Oden, p. 243.
20. Oden, p. 244.
21. Oden, p. 245.

Knowledge of the interaction of mind and body goes back at least to the fifth century B.C., but we now have scientific confirmation of this interaction. As the pastor enables patients to realize the forgiveness of God, to know inner peace, and to have a sense of control over their lives, patients will have a greater likelihood of regaining health. Research indicates that the ability to control the way one looks at demanding or stressful situations and how one reacts to them will determine whether the effects of stress are bad or good. If there was any doubt in a pastor's mind about the importance of pastoral care of the sick, this should make it clear.

The role of humor and a positive attitude in promoting healing is being emphasized more since medical science has the tools to evaluate the biochemical changes brought about by positive or negative feelings in patients. I have elaborated on this relationship between humor and healing in my book *Humor and Healing* (see bibliography). The theological meaning of humor is described in an essay by H. A. Williams thus:

> God, we believe, accepts us, accepts all men, unconditionally, warts and all. Laughter is the purest form of our response to God's acceptance of us. For when I laugh at myself I accept myself and when I laugh at other people in genuine mirth I accept them. Self-acceptance in laughter is the very opposite of self-satisfaction or pride. For in my laughter I accept myself not because I am some sort of super-person but precisely because I'm not. There is nothing funny about a super-person. There is everything funny about a man who thinks he is. In laughing at my own claims to

importance or regard I receive myself in a sort of loving forgiveness which is an echo of God's forgiveness of me. In much conventional contrition there is a selfishness and pride which are scarcely hidden. In our desperate self-concern we blame ourselves for not being the super-person we think we really are. But in laughter we sit light to ourselves. That is why laughter is the purest form of our response to God.[22]

The caring pastor will seek to enable the patient to respond to God with laughter on many occasions. And the pastor will help determine when and what kind of humor is appropriate.

The best humor is the spontaneous humor that arises out of the situation, says Victor Borge, who asserts that "A smile is the shortest distance between two people." This manual seeks to enable pastor and patient to discover the many avenues of healing God offers, especially the avenue of humor!

22. H. A. Williams, "Tensions," cited in Ruben P. Job and Norman Shawchuck, *A Guide to Prayer for Ministers and Other Servants* (Nashville: The Upper Room, 1987), pp. 239-40.

PART II

PASTORAL CARE FOR
SPECIFIC TYPES OF PATIENTS

5

THE AIDS PATIENT AND ASSOCIATES

The Surgeon General's report on AIDS (Acquired Immune Deficiency Syndrome) describes the disease in this way:

When a person is sick with AIDS he/she is in the final stages of a series of health problems caused by a virus (germ) that can be passed from one person to another chiefly during sexual contact or through the sharing of intravenous drug needles and syringes used for "shooting" drugs. Scientists have named the AIDS virus HIV or HTLV III or LAV. These abbreviations stand for information denoting a virus that attacks white blood cells (T-Lymphocytes) in the human blood. . . . The AIDS virus attacks a person's immune system and damages his/her ability to fight other disease. Without a functioning immune system to ward off other germs, he/she now becomes vulnerable to becoming infected by bacteria, protozoa, fungi, and other viruses and malignancies, which may cause life-threatening illness, such as pneumonia, meningitis, and cancer.

There is presently no cure for AIDS. There is presently no vaccine to prevent AIDS.

When the AIDS virus enters the blood stream, it begins to attack certain white blood cells (T-Lymphocytes). Substances called antibodies are produced by the body. These antibodies can be detected in the blood by a simple test, usually two weeks to three months after infection. Even before the antibody test is positive, the victim can pass the virus to others by methods that will be explained.

Once an individual is infected, there are several possibilities. Some people may remain well but even so they are able to infect others. Others may develop a disease that is less serious (ARC). In some people the protective immune system may be destroyed by the virus and then other germs (bacteria, protozoa, fungi and other viruses) and cancers that ordinarily would never get a foothold cause "opportunistic disease" — using the *opportunity* of lowered resistance to infect and destroy. Some of the most common are *Pneumocystis carinii* pneumonia and tuberculosis. Individuals infected with the AIDS viruses may also develop certain types of cancers such as Kaposi's sarcoma. These infected people have classic AIDS. Evidence shows that the AIDS virus may also attack the nervous system, causing damage to the brain. . . .

Some symptoms and signs of AIDS and the "opportunistic infections" may include a persistent cough and fever associated with shortness of breath or difficulty breathing and may be the symptoms of *Pneumocystis carinii* pneumonia. Multiple purplish blotches and bumps on the skin may be a sign of Kaposi's sarcoma. The AIDS virus in all infected people is essentially the same; the reactions of individuals may differ.[1]

1. C. Everett Koop, *Surgeon General's Report on Acquired Immune*

The report points out that everyday life does not present any risk of infection, and one cannot get AIDS from casual social contact. The pastor, in making a call on persons with AIDS, will not contract the illness from handshakes, hugs, social kisses, tears, coughs, or sneezes, according to the report. Knowledge of how the disease is and is not transmitted is an important asset for the pastor in ministering to AIDS patients and their associates.

The Surgeon General's report states that, although the AIDS virus is found in several body fluids, a person acquires the virus "during sexual contact with an infected person's blood or semen and possibly vaginal secretions. The virus then enters a person's blood stream through the rectum, vagina, or penis."[2] Some persons with hemophilia have been infected with the AIDS virus through either blood transfusions or the use of blood products that help the blood to clot. Transfusions are now being screened to prevent the spread of AIDS in this way. A woman infected with the AIDS virus who becomes pregnant is likely to develop ARC or classic AIDS, and she can pass the virus to her unborn child, who probably will die from the disease. For further details, refer to the full text of the Surgeon General's report and other reliable sources of information. New discoveries are being made almost daily, and pastors should keep informed in order to provide responsible ministry to patients and their associates.

Deficiency Syndrome (Washington, D.C.: U.S. Department of Health and Human Services, 1986), pp. 9-12.

2. Koop, p. 16.

Pastoral Care Needed

The immediate effect of a diagnosis of AIDS often conspires to undermine self-esteem, especially if fears about personal rejection are experienced. There may be reduced financial security and employment options, or even career loss. AIDS patients (*not* "victims") may become confused about what to do and how best to do it. Suicidal responses sometimes occur, and it is important for a sense of stability to be achieved. If you note indications of suicidal thoughts, this information should be given to the physician and referral made, if advisable. Patients change the way they react with others. Anxiety may lead to overdependence on hospital staff or caregivers at home. Lovers and family members may become frustrated and exhausted with having to stay with anxious patients who become hysterical when left alone. This can disrupt home life and business activities for associates of the patients.

Anxiety also can have the opposite effect, causing patients to reject all offers of emotional assistance as they seek complete self-determination and independence. Patients also are subject to anxiety expressed in hypochondria, seeing every small physical ailment as a sign of deterioration. Those in low-risk groups, the "worried well," may show abnormal fears of contagion. Anger against the disease can become displaced, aimed instead against the staff and close associates. Relationships that formerly were close may be disrupted, though this displaced anger should not be taken personally by associates or by the pastor.

The patients may feel guilt, that they are being punished for sins or past behavior. This can lead to bitterness, frustration, and rejection of those close in the past.

Depression is also a factor. Patients may feel that they deserve to have AIDS and may become withdrawn, leaving associates feeling helpless and frustrated. The great stress may bring about personality changes, disorientation, memory loss, poor concentration, speech and visual disorders, and loss of bodily control. Ataxia, or the inability to coordinate voluntary muscular movements, may occur.

If you are involved in the decision as to who should be told about the positive diagnosis, seek experienced counsel. Be aware of the impact on the patient's family, since some parents may be learning for the first time of their child's homosexuality or drug abuse, and major conflicts and prejudices may arise. You may want to consult with the chaplain of the hospital to ask for help in talking with the parents and associates.

Humor can be used to help deal with depression and develop a more hopeful, positive outlook for the AIDS patient.

Books and articles on pastoral care of AIDS patients and their associates are now appearing. *Mortal Fear* by John Snow (Cambridge, Mass.: Cowley Publications, 1987) deals with how to preach about AIDS and counsel people affected by AIDS. *AIDS,* by Earl E. Shelp, Ronald H. Sunderland, and Peter W. A. Mansell (New York: Pilgrim Press, 1987) provides useful information through stories about AIDS and the obligation of the church.

Prayer

O God, whose compassion is unbounded and whose mercy is endless, we come to you with trusting hearts, knowing you are already present with us. We pray for *N.,* asking that you be especially near to *(him/her)* and reassure *(him/her)* of your love that never ends. We pray for the members of the health-care team who are caring for *N.* We pray for family and close friends and ask for your presence and power. You know our needs, our fears, our anxieties, our hopes. We bring them to you in prayer, trusting in Christ, who died for us that we might be forgiven and have eternal life. In his name we pray. Amen.

Scripture

- Psalm 23 (p. 171 below)
- Psalm 40, selected verses
- Psalm 121 (p. 172 below)
- Psalm 139:1-14, 23-24
- Lamentations 3:55-58 (p. 175 below)
- 2 Corinthians 4:7-9 (p. 180 below)
- 2 Corinthians 12:9-10
- 1 John 1:5-9

6

THE BURN PATIENT

A burn patient calls on the resources of a hospital in a fuller measure than probably any other patient. Caring for the patient can be very demanding and expensive. The effects of burns are devastating, especially for the very young and the older person. When admitted to the hospital, patients are often in a state of severe physical pain and shock. They usually feel as if they have come through a nightmare, recalling the flames and desperate attempts at rescue.

During the acute phase, which may last six to eight weeks or even longer, a patient's chief question is "Will I survive?" And many patients do not survive. Pain and prolonged discomfort are a persistent aspect of burns; much crying and many moans, screams, and shouts for relief are heard in the burn unit.

When patients realize that death is not imminent, the mood usually shifts from a state of anxiety to depression. Patients may feel that they will be in the hospital forever. And young people often misinterpret and magnify their injuries. Patients wonder what handicaps will result from the burns, what they will be able to do, when they can return home. Many have traumatic memories that need healing and fears about the future related to the disfiguring scars.

They may struggle with a state of helplessness, and dependency behavior is likely to develop. Guilt may be expressed by those who have broken moral standards regarding drinking and sexual conduct. Parents of children who have been burned sustain a high degree of guilt. A majority of patients suffer from depression, and many need to be healed of their traumatic memories of the burn accident.

Treatment may call for long-term rehabilitation and can turn what at first seemed to be an acute situation into a chronic one, going on year after year. A number of people may be involved in this long-term treatment, and the pastor should become acquainted with them when possible, in order to work more closely as a team member in the rehabilitation process.

PASTORAL CARE NEEDED

The care you can give will grow out of your own faith and life, bringing this to bear on the needs of the burn patient.

Building on Jeremiah's questions, "Is there no balm in Gilead? Is there no physician there?" (8:22), Claude Deal, Jr., writes that the balm the minister can apply to the burn patient "will depend upon the skills he has acquired in making these healing agents [pastoral relationships] a positive and concrete reality."[1]

A minister's own psychological reaction is a basic issue in offering pastoral care. Guard against showing feelings

1. Claude Deal, Jr., "Balm for Burned Patients," in *Pastor and Patient,* ed. Richard Dayringer (New York: Jason Aronson, 1982), p. 124.

of revulsion at the sight of a burn patient, especially since the patient may have lost self-esteem. The pastor may want to talk over the planned visit with the hospital chaplain to prepare for seeing a patient.

The pastor may use appropriate humor with the burn patient to help deal with anxiety and later with depression. This needs to be done carefully if laughing will cause pain. Using humor can be a way of expressing care and creating a more positive attitude.

A sense of hope will help the pastor minister to the patient. Give nonverbal communication by the use of body contact, with proper precautions for avoiding infection. A soothing touch on a nonburned hand or forehead may be very helpful. Help the patient deal with anxiety and despair by offering hope, expectancy, and encouragement to endure the pain with God's help. Sharing prayer, Scripture, and religious experiences with the patient can be very supportive.

Pastors also should try to deal with the *causes* of many burns — poor housing, inadequate supervision of children, unsafe heating facilities. The mobilization of community efforts to *prevent* burns should be a high priority.

PRAYER

God of healing, hope, and love, we come to you in prayer, trusting your promises to be with us in our pain and suffering as well as in our peace and joy. We thank you for this hospital and those who work on the health-care teams. We pray for them as they care for *N.* and the other patients here. May the balm of your presence be with *N.* and give *(him/her)* healing and hope. Relieve the anxiety about tomorrow. Help us to accept what cannot be changed, grant us courage to change what can be changed, and give us the wisdom to know the difference. Amen.

SCRIPTURE

- Psalm 22, selected verses
- Psalm 23 (p. 171 below)
- Proverbs 17:22 (p. 173 below)
- Isaiah 40:28-31 (p. 173 below)
- Isaiah 41:10
- Jeremiah 30:17
- Luke 17:11-19
- Philippians 4:1, 4-7 (p. 181 below)

7

THE CANCER PATIENT

Cancer will affect one of every five people in America; it will take the life of one out of eight. It is sometimes a slow, insidious disease, one that may be cured or contained in one part of the body only to appear again in another. Cancer follows a crisis-ridden course, taking jogs and turns for the better or for worse. It often elicits guilt and provokes doubt.

The Hospice movement, which began in England, is enabling many incurable cancer patients to remain at home surrounded by family and friends, rather than dying isolated in a hospital. While serving primarily cancer patients, Hospice also plans and provides care for other terminally ill patients such as those with heart problems or Alzheimer's disease. I have observed the positive difference Hospice can make in the quality of life of the dying patient. For information, write or call The National Hospice Organization, 1901 North Ft. Myer Drive, Arlington, VA 22209; Tel. (703) 243-5900.

Cancer goes through several stages: (1) the initial stage, in which neoplastic disease has been diagnosed; (2) the advancing stage, in which metastasis, or spreading, of the cancer is confirmed; and (3) the terminal stage, in which cancer cannot be controlled and death will result.

Most of us assume that we will go on living forever, in

control of our lives. Cancer shatters this assumption. It frightens not only the patient but also family and friends. Each wonders "Am I next?" This is particularly true of family members, since cancer seems more likely to run in certain families.

The effect of cancer has been compared to looking through a camera lens. Before cancer, one sees life with a fairly broad vision, and all is clear. When cancer is diagnosed, the view becomes unfocused and scattered. Everything "out there" in life seems jumbled and cluttered. When treatment is started, a new clarity of vision appears, but with a narrower focus. A recurrence of cancer knocks the camera out of focus again. If the patient reaches the terminal stage, the focus is close-up, and peripheral vision is blurred. Life is seen in a different way: Now only the most valued things of life are clear.

Since various kinds of cancer and their occurrence at various ages affect persons differently, and breakthroughs in the control or cure are being made, this brief overview will give only a short summary. A cancer residency program or other training will enable pastors to better understand the nature of cancer and what is being done in medical research and with patients and their families throughout the country. Such programs often are developed and carried out by the pastoral services department of a hospital and jointly sponsored by the local chapter of the American Cancer Society. Various teachers in the health-care team that deal with cancer help pastors and chaplains learn how to work together more effectively.

PASTORAL CARE NEEDED

While cancer may be arrested or controlled in various stages for long periods of time, the initial stage moves patients to talk freely, honestly, and repeatedly about the diagnosis. As the cancer advances, hope gives way to fear, truth to veiled statements, and faith in physicians is shaken or abandoned. Silence is common in the terminal stage, and patients need various kinds of support from different persons. Depression may occur at any stage and should be dealt with by physicians and pastors.

Leroy G. Kerney outlines the following ministry, which begins in understanding but must move beyond to other forms of involvement:

1. Be present with the patient. The cancer patient often fears being abandoned, especially in the terminal stage. The "silent sound of love" is basic in ministry to cancer patients.

2. Give the patient opportunity for dialogue. Help can come from putting feelings into words. When the person expresses in words what is being thought and felt, there is healing. The patient may be ambivalent about many things — living or dying, feeling strong or weak.

3. Help the patient celebrate life. Through the use of Scripture, prayer, and the sacraments, the pastor can help the patient, both alone and in community with family and friends, to focus on the religious meaning of life and on trust, love, and hope.[1]

Alden Sproull points out that growth and intimacy can

---

1. Leroy G. Kerney, "Ministering to Cancer Patients," in *Pastor and Patient,* ed. Richard Dayringer (New York: Jason Aronson, 1982), p. 164.

occur when strong negative feelings such as revolt, resentment, hatred, rage, and bitterness can be expressed. The diagnosis of cancer brings people to clarify the values of life.

> The chaplain brings a symbolic and personal presence to this quest for the basic issues of life. Through this presence the chaplain tries to meet some of the obvious needs for respect, love, appreciation, listening, and hope. . . . Such a ministry can impact the values and deepen the spirituality of the one who ministers. . . . Indeed, those who minister become co-sojourners in the most intimate, challenging experiences of life.[2]

John Robert McFarland, a recovering cancer patient and minister, has shared his feelings about cancer in his inspirational book entitled *Now That I Have Cancer I Am Whole* (see bibliography). In brief reflections on his experience with cancer, McFarland has written honestly about his feelings in sections such as "When You Are Bald and Strangely Beautiful (Treatment)," "When It's Time for New Thinking (Attitude Adjustment)," and "When It's Time to Look Inside (Dealing with Our Feelings)." This book will help family members, pastors, and patients in dealing with cancer.

Lawrence A. Siebert, a psychologist, has researched and written a pamphlet about the "survivor personality." Such a person is his or her own master, tenacious, creative, and adaptable. Many people who have survived cancer have learned to convert misfortune into good luck.

---

2. Alden Sproull, "The Voices on Cancer Care: A Lens Unfocused and Narrowed," in *Hospital Ministry: The Role of the Chaplain Today,* ed. Lawrence E. Holst (New York: Crossroad, 1985), p. 126.

People who are life's best survivors get to be the way they are by gaining strength from life's trials. When you are hit by adversity and misfortune you have a choice. You can dwell on your version of "if only . . ." or you can handle the situation so that things turn out well for yourself and others. Whatever you are trying to cope with could turn out to be the best thing that ever happened to you.[3]

The pastor who works with those who have cancer, heart trouble, or other kinds of illnesses may find Siebert's findings useful in helping patients to cope.

Humor is being used effectively with cancer patients to develop a more positive attitude. Dr. Bernie Siegel has developed a program for cancer patients and has written on the subject (see bibliography). Cancer seems especially vulnerable to a change in attitude toward life and a change in life-style. Humor can help in this process.

PRAYER

Loving God unto whom all hearts are open, all desires known, and from whom no secrets are hid, we come to you in prayer because you have already come to us by your Spirit to move us to seek you. When you seem far away, we know you are yet nearer to us than hands or feet or breathing itself. We pray for *N.*, asking that you give *(him/her)* strength and courage to face this illness

---

3. Lawrence A. Siebert, *Developing Your Talent for Serendipity: How to Gain Strength from Difficult and Stressful Situations* (privately printed; available from P. O. Box 505, Portland, OR 97207).

with faith and hope. We pray for the members of the health-care team as they care for *N.* Grant them wisdom and healing power. Enable us to see more clearly the things that are really important in life: love for you, our God, and love for one another. We pray through Christ. Amen.

SCRIPTURE

- Job 42:1-6
- Psalm 6:1-4, 7, 9
- Psalm 23 (p. 171 below)
- Isaiah 55:10-13 (p. 174 below)
- Jeremiah 17:7-8, 14 (p. 174 below)
- Lamentations 3:55-58 (p. 175 below)
- Mark 5:24-34
- 2 Corinthians 4:7-9 (p. 180 below)
- Philippians 4:8 (p. 181 below)

8

CHILDREN

Pastors should read some of the outstanding books on children and illness, preferably *before* being called in to minister to a child who is ill. Andrew D. Lester, who wrote *Pastoral Care with Children in Crises*, has edited a more recent sourcebook for ministry with children in crisis, *When Children Suffer*. John B. Hesch, a Roman Catholic priest, has written *Clinical Pastoral Care for Hospitalized Children and Their Families*. In addition, five chapters in the book *Pastor and Patient*, edited by Richard Dayringer, and a chapter by Jim Arnold in *Hospital Ministry*, edited by Lawrence E. Holst, provide excellent insights and guidance for pastoral care for children and their families.

Pastors who minister to children need to learn to communicate on their level. You may need to make it clear who you are and what the visit is all about. Jim Arnold tells about visiting an eleven-year-old boy scheduled for elective surgery. They watched television for a while, then Arnold asked the boy if he knew what a chaplain, pastor, priest, or rabbi is. During a commercial the boy replied, "I know what a pastor is. That's the place where they keep the cows." Arnold asked to be the boy's friend and they talked about being in the hospital and the coming surgery.[1]

1. Jim Arnold, "The Voices on Pediatrics: Walking with Children

Out of this experience came the observation that children can identify with people — human beings — but they have great difficulty identifying with "pastors." Thus an initial task is to become an understanding, caring friend to the child. A minister may find it refreshing to drop the clerical role for a few minutes and just be another person who likes to play games or watch a favorite television program.

A hand puppet can be very helpful in talking with children. While some pastors may not feel comfortable doing this, there are rewards for using puppets with young children. Older children may draw pictures or write a story to tell about their feelings. Once the pastor has established a rapport with the child, the door is opened to carry through an appropriate ministry.

Children have the same feelings adults do: fear, loneliness, guilt, anger, joy, happiness. Arnold points out that "effective ministry with hospitalized children, adolescents, and their families comes out of a knowledge and understanding of their world, particularly of how illness impacts their total life experiences."[2] Since hospital ministry is crisis ministry, the patient's needs may be described as hope, trust, love, acceptance, and caring. Simple religious words and symbols should be used in communicating with children. But the basic communication is not through words but in *trustworthy relationships.*

Harold Buller points out that ministry to a child falls

and Parents," in *Hospital Ministry,* ed. Lawrence E. Holst (New York: Crossroad, 1985), p. 92.

2. Arnold, p. 94.

into three main areas: (1) a direct person-to-person relationship, (2) through the parents, and (3) through the hospital staff. The pastor can help prepare the child for hospitalization by encouraging the parents to be honest in explaining what to expect. The pastor, says Buller, should begin ministry with an ill child by remembering that the child is already emotionally aware and has begun "to deal with the basic affects — love, sex, rage, fear. It is only as he or she is helped to cope with these in the hospital environment that his/her illness will become an experience upon which he/she can build. If he/she cannot control these emotions at this time he/she will be blocked from receiving and assimilating new stimuli that help him/her to grow."[3] The pastor may want to share with the parents one or more articles or books about children and illness, to give them a better understanding of their child's feelings and behavior.

While most children who enter the hospital stay for a relatively brief time, others suffer from chronic, life-threatening diseases. Whether the illness is acute or chronic, the child suffers from "hospitalization crisis," which involves the anxiety of separation from parents and siblings. Adolescents in the hospital usually find this a time of learning to cope, getting into hospital routine, tolerating it, and getting out as soon as possible. They may become bored by it all and work through pain, confusion, and anxiety, then try to forget it all as soon as possible.

3. Harold Buller, "Ministry to Hospitalized Children," in *Pastor and Patient,* ed. Richard Dayringer (New York: Jason Aronson, 1982), p. 218.

Pastoral Care Needed

In the case of the chronically ill child, the basic question of theodicy is usually raised by the parents and family. (See Chapter 4, "The Patient and Illness," for a discussion of theodicy.) One of the faith answers to this problem of apparent evil permitted by a good and all-powerful God is found in the twenty-third psalm: "I fear no evil; for thou art with me." God's presence with the chronically ill child and family members is the basic assurance needed. Arnold says, "God's presence is felt most vividly through persons who walk alongside. *Ministry then becomes walking with children and their parents through the journey of testing, diagnosis, treatment, perhaps relapse, even death.*"[4]

Gary Brock points out that effective ministry to the chronically ill child takes both *time* and *commitment,* and four areas of knowledge are needed:

1. Know the sick child. The child cannot be known in isolation from the overall impact of the illness. Be aware of its immediate physical and emotional effects. [Focus your attention on the child.] Be sure you bring a part of you to the conversation. . . . Be sure you leave the blessings of the church. If you pray, pray *with* the child and *not about* him or her.

2. Know the family. . . . Being present to listen to the parents' concerns, their direct or subtle pleas for help, asking both the difficult and the sensitive questions — these are the kinds of things upon which a pastoral relationship is built. Families in crisis become very narrowly

4. Arnold, p. 99.

— sometimes dangerously — focused. The minister brings the fresh, healing air of a new perspective. . . .

3. Know the immediate needs of both. The minister may need to take on the role of advocate. Is what the child needs readily available? . . . With the role of advocate also comes the role of teacher. Given the tendency of medicine to focus on particular areas of the body or on specific limitations, the minister must consistently remind all involved that a whole child is at risk. In order to be helpful, the minister needs to have a working knowledge of what is happening to this child. . . .

4. Know yourself. Why are you there: As pastor? As friend? As stranger? What can you bring them that no one else can — personally or professionally? How do they interpret your role as representative of God in what is happening to them? . . . Sometimes children and parents get angry or disappointed with God. Can you handle this being directed at you? What are your own reactions, to illness in general and to sick children in particular? Some ministers simply are not able to enter into this kind of care. If this is true, be honest about it and let someone in the congregation minister in your behalf. Parents appreciate honesty much more than being ignored.[5]

Brock also discusses what to do if you move on to another church or job and are no longer pastor to the

5. Gary Brock, "The Chronically Ill Child," in *When Children Suffer,* ed. Andrew D. Lester (Philadelphia: Westminster Press, 1987), pp. 122-23.

chronically ill child and parents."Leave-taking must receive careful attention. The age of the child and length of the relationship will determine what needs to be said."[6] The suggestions offered can be useful also in terminating pastoral relationships with other very sick parishioners.

First, take time to explain why you are leaving, since children are usually aware that people move and take other jobs. Next, show on a map where you will be going and have a picture of the new church or hospital where you will be working. Tell the child you will write, and be sure to follow up on this promise! Try to maintain contact, since illness-related crises may occur. Anticipate your own pain over the leave-taking. And make the necessary introductions of the person who will be assuming pastoral care of the child and family.

Brock, director of pastoral care in a large university teaching hospital, summarizes the ministry a chronically ill child needs: "Sick children are fragile. Their parents are especially fragile. Assumptions underlying one's pastoral care must be carefully considered. A cautious sensitivity must inform each visit. As a representative of God, be mindful of the 'kind' of God you represent."[7]

The pastor will find that children respond to humor and play, and these may be the best ways to relate to the child. Humor shows that one cares and creates community.

6. Brock, p. 114.
7. Brock, p. 114.

Prayer

Our loving heavenly Father, we pray together, asking that your power and presence may be with N. We thank you for Jesus, who loved children. He said, "Let the children come to me," and he put his hands on them and blessed them. We thank you for the doctors, nurses, and others who are caring for N. here in the hospital. We pray for them and ask that you give them divine healing power. We pray for N.'s parent(s) and family. Watch over and care for them. Now we ask your blessing upon N., and may *(he/she)* know that nothing can separate us from your love in Christ Jesus our Lord. In his name we pray. Amen.

Scripture

- Psalm 23 (p. 171 below)
- Isaiah 40:28-31 (p. 173 below)
- Matthew 4:23-25
- Mark 10:46-52

9

THE CORONARY PATIENT

In ministering to the coronary patient, you may encounter some of the most challenging issues of life — issues that will move you to reexamine your own life, values, goals, and stewardship in light of our common mortality. The heart is viewed as the sustainer of life. As of this writing, no artificial heart has been devised that will give long-term service in replacing the natural heart. Thus threat to the heart is a threat to life. As a result of coronary disease, people often make significant life-style changes.

The pastor has an opportunity to minister by being an empathetic listener, a confronter of reality, and a guide in helping to interpret the inner, spiritual pilgrimage of the heart patient. The questions of God's sovereign rule, of our mortality and limitations, of values and goals, may be subjects of reflection, with the pastor's guidance. The way in which the patient responds to these issues and others can have a profound effect on the healing process.

The important role of emotions in coronary disease is pointed up by researchers in Israel who "studied ten thousand men with risk factors for angina pectoris — abnormal heart rhythms and high anxiety levels." The research revealed that one of the other "most accurate predictor[s] of chest pains was a 'No' answer to the question, 'Does your wife show you her love?' "[1]

Bernie Siegel quotes a fellow physician, Franz Alexander: "The fact that the mind rules the body is, in spite of its neglect by biology and medicine, the most fundamental fact which we know about the process of life."[2]

Siegel says "exceptional patients," about 15 to 20 percent of the people he has studied in working primarily with cancer patients, "refuse to be victims. They educate themselves and become specialists in their own care. They question the doctor because they want to understand their treatment and participate in it. They demand dignity, personhood, and control, no matter what the course of the disease."[3]

To determine whether you are an "exceptional person," Siegel poses this question: "Do you want to live to be a hundred?" People who say "Yes" from the gut, "with no ifs, ands, or buts . . . have what psychologists call an *inner locus of control*. They do not fear the future or external events. They know that happiness is an inside job."[4]

I knew a parishioner who lived to be 104, the oldest DuPont Company pensioner at the time of his death. He maintained a vital interest in sports on television, kept up correspondence with friends, and had a positive, hopeful attitude toward the future. He had found happiness

1. Bernie S. Siegel, *Love, Medicine and Miracles: Lessons Learned About Self-Healing from a Surgeon's Experience with Exceptional Patients* (New York: Harper & Row, 1986), p. 183.

2. Siegel, p. 1.

3. Siegel, p. 24.

4. Siegel, pp. 25-26.

within, in spite of the earlier death of his wife of many years and the illness of his only child, a daughter, who was confined to a wheelchair.

Robert Stromberg outlines three stages of coronary illness: (1) prehospitalization, (2) hospitalization, and (3) posthospitalization.[5] No typical set of symptoms will clearly indicate heart disease, and this often makes self-diagnosis difficult. Denial of symptoms is the most typical response; even physicians and cardiologists have been known to deny their own symptoms. But time is crucial. Most deaths from heart disease occur because of delays in getting adequate medical attention. Research shows that of those who reach the hospital and get help, most survive.

In the hospital the patient undergoes testing and evaluation, which may produce considerable anxiety. The patient may imagine the worst, or may continue to deny that anything is wrong. Be aware of the challenge to the person's faith in God and others at this point.

After being in the hospital, the heart patient reflects on the meaning of the illness and may gain a new perspective on life. Questions often plague the patient during this time: Who am I? What can I still do? Will they still love me? Will I be productive again? Will they stand by me? Will I have another heart attack?

Humor can be especially helpful for the coronary patient as she or he deals with depression and creating a new life-style which is more relaxed and playful.

5. Robert Stromberg, "The Voices on Coronary Care," in *Hospital Ministry,* ed. Lawrence E. Holst (New York: Crossroad, 1985), p. 127.

Pastoral Care Needed

Denial is a normal and healthy coping mechanism for coronary patients. Studies indicate that people with healthy denial systems are better survivors of crises, but denial can be unhealthy if it prevents a person from eventually dealing with the seriousness of the crisis. Work with the physician, chaplain, and family in confronting and challenging the prolonged denial that is unhealthy.

Fear and anxiety also are factors. There may be fear — not of dying, but of being an invalid. Help the patient deal with fear and anxiety by talking about fears and developing security in God and in other persons through prayer and Scripture.

Anger, shame, and guilt also must be dealt with. Anger may not be expressed toward God or physicians but instead toward the food served in the hospital or restrictions placed on the patient. The patient may feel shame because he or she cannot be productive at this time and is dependent on others.

Guilt is another factor. Some guilt may be neurotic, but as Stromberg points out, heart patients need to deal with some real guilt when they learn that they are responsible for the life-style which contributed to their heart condition.

Patients will be reminded that smoking cigarettes, poor nutritional habits, lack of regular exercise, uncontrolled blood pressure and diabetes, and stressful life-styles may have contributed to their heart disease. Accepting responsibility for the consequences of those "sins" may be a painful but redemptive experience. . . . The challenge of making life-style changes is one of the most difficult issues facing the coronary patient. . . . The most difficult challenge facing the coronary patient, however, is the need to change personality traits that may have been responsible for their career success (i.e., driving competitiveness, perfectionism).[6]

Be alert for a patient's feelings of emptiness and depression. The coronary patient may feel worthless, express self-doubt, lack energy and the ability to concentrate, and be unable to cope with this depression by activity, travel, or exercise.

Watch also for a sense of depersonalization and feelings of isolation. The patient may look inward and search for meaning and, in doing so, feel lonely. Heart patients need to be with people who will understand and appreciate the struggles they are undergoing.

Recovered coronary patients may feel a great sense of gratitude to God. Be sensitive to this and help patients and their families celebrate the recovery. They may want to offer prayers of thanks and may appreciate psalms of gratitude and hymns of thanksgiving. Patients usually feel a strong sense of well-being and hopefulness as they regain health. Help them find ways to give to others what they have received during their illness — love that is unconditional and caring, expressed in both word and act.

PRAYER

Gracious God who has loved us with an everlasting love, a love that will not let us go, we praise you, we adore you,

6. Stromberg, pp. 132-34.

we thank you. We join together in praying for *N.*, asking that Jesus the divine Physician may bring healing through the work of the earthly physicians, nurses, and other members of the health-care team. We pray that your Spirit may work in *N.*'s life to give courage, faith, and hope in this time of illness. We thank you for the loving support of family and friends. We ask your blessing upon each of them and upon *N.*, your servant. We pray in Christ's name. Amen.

SCRIPTURE

- Psalm 23 (p. 171 below)
- Psalm 27, selected verses
- Psalm 34
- Psalm 100 (p. 172 below)
- Psalm 103
- Psalm 121 (p. 172 below)
- Proverbs 17:22 (p. 173 below)
- 2 Corinthians 4:7-9 (p. 180 below)
- 2 Corinthians 12:9-10
- Philippians 4:10-13, 19 (p. 181 below)

10

MINISTRY TO THE DYING

Ministry to the dying, and to their families, is one of the most sacred privileges of the pastor. It is one time when many people especially want their pastor near. Your effectiveness in this ministry will be based on how well you have integrated into life what is believed about death and about life.

Leroy Joesten, a hospital chaplain, writes: "We have learned that unless pastors are at peace with their own mortality and its vast implications, they are not free to accompany others in their dying."[1]

Carl Nighswonger, in a similar vein, says that "fulfillment in death can come only when one's life perspective adequately answers the question of meaning and purpose in the realm of destiny. Basic to the Christian ministry is a life perspective which offers such an interpretation. The revelation of God in Jesus Christ discloses the reality of God's love for [us] and reveals his concern for man's destiny."[2]

1. Leroy Joesten, "The Voices of the Dying and Bereaved," in *Hospital Ministry,* ed. Lawrence E. Holst (New York: Crossroad, 1985), p. 149.
2. Carl Nighswonger, "Ministering to the Dying," in *Pastor and Patient,* ed. Richard Dayringer (New York: Jason Aronson, 1982), p. 185.

Denial is a natural emotional response. It protects the ego and is necessary if the person is to distinguish between the inevitability of death and the imminence of death. Family and friends are torn between being forced by circumstances to surrender the dying person and being forced by the emotional ties of love to hold on to the patient as long as possible. Loved ones often tell dying persons how much they are needed, that life can't go on without them, and they encourage them to fight to the very end.

Nighswonger points up the twofold sting of death: (1) the threat of death and its meaning for life, and (2) the grief that results from being separated from all one has known in life: family, friends, work, play. He outlines the five major dramas in dying as the person passes through the valley of the shadow:

1. Denial vs. Panic
2. Catharsis vs. Depression
3. Bargaining vs. Selling Out
4. Realistic Hope vs. Despair
5. Acceptance vs. Resignation[3]

The dying person may try to bargain for a cure and recovery, but if this is impossible the person may come to hope simply that the dying will not be prolonged or give much pain or expense to the family. In the final stage the person may be able to affirm death as the natural fulfillment of life, the completion of its meaning and purpose. "Though he may withdraw from those around him, one

3. Nighswonger, p. 187.

senses a spirit of peace and equanimity," says Nighs-wonger.[4] Families can accept death when the dying person has been able to find meaning. And dying persons can conclude life with a sense of "It is finished" and let go, knowing that their life pilgrimage was not in vain.

Research reveals that persons with six months to live have a greater sense of humor than the average person. They often joke about death as a way of dealing with their feelings. The pastor should not try to change the subject but rather follow the patient's feelings and respond appropriately. Humor about death with a dying child is not appropriate since a child's view of death is different from an adult's view. However, general humor may be one of the best ways to communicate with and support the dying child. It is *never* appropriate to use humor with the family of a dying adult or child.

THE DYING CHILD

When children die, their emotional reactions correspond to their maturity in years. By the age of five or six, a child has become aware, in a meaningful way, of death as the end of life. With younger children, pastoral care is pointed more toward the support of the family members. Carl Stephens, in writing about pastoral care of the dying child, divides childhood into three phases: (1) birth to age five; (2) age six to age ten; (3) age ten to adolescence.[5]

While the toddler and young child are aware of death

4. Nighswonger, p. 190.

5. Carl Stephens, "Pastoral Care for the Dying Child and His Family," in *Pastor and Patient,* p. 225.

and view it as natural, they are seldom aware of their own mortality. The young child realizes something is wrong and to be feared because of parental reaction. The pastor's role is to help the family with their emotional struggle.

During grade-school years, ages six to ten, the child knows that death means a final separation from life. He or she mourns the loss of life, family, friends. "He is sad and bitter because he does not want to go. He is lonely because he is traveling this journey alone," says Stephens.[6]

Adolescents live in a transitional world, moving between dependent childhood and independent adulthood. This age wants to live and to experience, but on the other hand death is fascinating because it is one of life's deeper experiences. Stephens describes this reaction:

> The lonely and dying adolescent may violently reject his parents, his family, and the adult members of the treatment team — not because he does not desperately want their understanding and support but because in reality he so much longs for their caring that he cannot allow himself to admit these feelings. He wishes so much to be cared for and protected that he dreads losing control over himself. He longs for understanding but so greatly fears the loss of his new independence that he has to force people away. However, the dying adolescent between ten and fifteen years may allow himself to be a child in the bosom of his family as death grows nearer, as long as he does not feel he is being treated disrespectfully. The minister can help the child and his family by making them understand this. Since

6. Stephens, p. 229.

the young adolescent has already a tendency to feel guilty as he tries to separate himself from his parents, he frequently sees death as confirmation that he has been bad. It is sensed as merited punishment.[7]

A firm belief in a loving, forgiving God is a strong source of strength and comfort for the adolescent facing death. Be aware of what religion means to the dying child and offer help at the level the child can use.

Pastoral Care Needed

The pastor can minister to the dying child in three ways, says Barbara J. Prescott-Ezickson: (1) Help the child "distinguish between correct and incorrect information." (2) "Admit that for some questions there are no answers." The tragic death of a child is a mystery beyond explanation. With parents or grandparents living, a child's death is especially devastating to all concerned. (3) "Be sensitive to the deeper needs these questions represent." By being honest with children and encouraging their questions we can support them as they arrive at conclusions that work for them.[8]

Prescott-Ezickson cites a wealth of helpful material for ministering to dying children. She mentions stories about Jesus and children, Jesus' grief over Lazarus, and Bible characters who prayed to God; passages that describe God's goodness and love, the Easter story, images of res-

7. Stephens, p. 230.

8. Barbara J. Prescott-Ezickson, "The Terminally Ill Child," *When Children Suffer,* ed. Andrew D. Lester (Philadelphia: Westminster Press, 1987), p. 112.

urrection, what happens after death, and what heaven is like. These give the dying child "a sense of reassurance. When these theological images are used appropriately and gently, in comfortable story form, they can be extremely meaningful for dying children."[9]

Whether ministering to a child or to an adult, "be a companion to the dying person and family in a very special way." The most important skill for ministry to the dying is the capacity for compassion, which should be developed continually throughout one's ministry. Gerald D. Calhoun, who directed pastoral care in a hospital for eight years, gives this guidance:

> Words become far less important than simple gestures and a shared silence. Sitting with a family, encouraging them to hold the hand of their loved one or to put a cold cloth on a perspiring forehead or to moisten parched lips with a little water; offering prayer, brief and not prolonged, or making a sign of the cross on the dying person's forehead; spelling a family member who needs to take a break or bringing coffee or soft drinks to refresh the family — each of these thoughtful gestures means more than a thousand words.
>
> [At the time of death] supporting them in touching the body and talking to it, protecting their privacy as each close relative may want to say good-bye separately and alone, putting an arm around a bereaved family member which might help them cry, and crying with them, if the tears are there, will speak profoundly of the chaplain's care for them and of the Lord's compassionate love.

9. Prescott-Ezickson, pp. 112-13.

Voicing a simple prayer after the family has had time to say good-bye and to comfort one another often brings closure to their vigil and gives them an invitation to separate themselves from the place of death.[10]

Families may appreciate joining hands around the bed of the deceased, along with nurses and friends, for a prayer of thanksgiving for the person's life and a commendation of the person to God's keeping. Words of comfort for the family should be included, and a brief Scripture passage (such as selections from John 14) may be read.

Calhoun advises the pastor to take seriously dying persons' premonitions about their death. They may have dreams in which deceased parents call the dying to join them.

The pastor may help dying persons by encouraging them to tell their life story. Many people can sum up their lives in a few stories from their past. In listening, the pastor can help the dying find peace, wholeness, completion of life, and acceptance of death.

Be supportive, too, of the family and friends as they grieve and "release" the dying. Grief causes pain, and the bereaved need understanding, patience, and acceptance. No matter how long a person may anticipate the death of a loved one, the actual moment is still a painful experience, though there may also be a deep sense of relief — both for self and for the person who died.

A dying person may want to discuss funeral plans, and sometimes the pastor is the only one willing to talk about

10. Gerald D. Calhoun, *Pastoral Companionship* (New York: Paulist Press, 1986), p. 107.

the approaching death. Planning for the funeral need not be morbid, but may be a means of accepting the reality of death, both by the dying person and by the family.[11]

The patient may want to receive Communion as death draws near, make a public profession of faith and be baptized, or reaffirm his or her faith in preparation for death. Rituals found in Part II of this manual may be adapted as required for particular persons and circumstances.

Prayer

Almighty God, be near to your servant *N.*, who lies here very weak, and comfort *(him/her)* with the promise of eternal life given in the resurrection of your Son Jesus Christ. Deliver your servant *N.*, O Lord Jesus Christ, from all evil and set *(him/her)* free from every bond. May *(he/she)* rest with all your saints in the eternal habitations where you live with the Father and Holy Spirit, one God forever and ever. We remember the faith of the psalmist: "I will both lie down and sleep in peace; for you alone, O Lord, make me lie down in safety" (Ps. 4:8). We thank you for the assurance in Scripture that nothing can separate us from your love in Christ Jesus our Lord. Hear our prayer in the words of the hymn:

Abide with me; fast falls the eventide;
The darkness deepens; Lord, with me abide!
When other helpers fail and comforts flee,
Help of the helpless, O abide with me.

11. See my *Funeral Manual* (Grand Rapids: William B. Eerdmans, 1994).

We pray as Jesus taught us, saying:

> Our Father who art in heaven,
> hallowed be thy name.
> Thy kingdom come,
> thy will be done
>   on earth as it is in heaven.
> Give us this day our daily bread.
> And forgive us our *(trespasses/debts)*
>   as we forgive *(those who trespass against us/*
>   *our debtors).*
> And lead us not into temptation,
>   but deliver us from evil.
> For thine is the kingdom, and the power, and
>   the glory,
>   for ever and ever. *Amen.*

SCRIPTURE

- Numbers 6:24-26 (p. 171 below)
- Psalm 23 (p. 171 below)
- Psalm 27, selected verses
- Psalm 46
- Psalm 91:1-4, 14-16
- Matthew 26:36-39
- John 3:16-18 (p. 177 below)
- Romans 8:31-39 (p. 179 below)
- Romans 14:7-8
- Revelation 21:1-5 (p. 182 below)

11

THE EMOTIONALLY ILL PATIENT

A pastor who makes calls in the psychiatric unit of a hospital or in a hospital for the emotionally ill needs to design a tailor-made ministry for each patient.

Because of the schedule for therapy, treatments, and various activities, the pastor should call ahead to the charge nurse to ask when the patient will be available for a visit. You may want to talk with the patient's physician and/or psychiatrist to inquire about the patient's needs and how you may help. A nurse, social worker, or other health-care team member may be able to give guidance in counseling the patient. You may find that the person's treatment calls for no visitors — not even the pastor — for a period of days or weeks. Pray for the patient, write notes, and be supportive of the family and friends during this time of isolation.

Many of those who are emotionally ill are depressed, and ministry to these patients needs to be shaped accordingly. Depression has been called "the common cold of mental illness" because of its frequency. Great strides have been made in recent years to relieve depression and effect changes within both the emotional life of patients and their relationships with others.

Willard Wagner points out that "patients suffering from intense depression have little ability to concentrate on anything other than the pain they are experiencing. Generally, this type of depression is seen as a biological condition requiring medical intervention; though there are also important psychosocial aspects, psychotherapy is often ineffective until the severe depression is relieved."[1] Depressions occur most often after the age of thirty; the incidence peaks between forty and sixty, then tapers off. If suicidal threats are expressed, these must be taken seriously. Be alert to such hints and consult with the patient's psychiatrist about the pastor's special role in supporting and treating the patient.

Joe Boone Abbott has described the symptoms of the depressed person, many of which may not be obvious to those outside the family until the depressive reaction is well on its way:

> It may begin with chronic fatigue coupled with restless sleep and loss of appetite. The effort needed to get started in the morning and the difficulty in controlling morbid thoughts adds to the growing distress. The person may then begin to awaken at 2 to 3 A.M. with disturbing dreams. Physical symptoms such as crying, weight loss, sleep disturbance, fatigue, constipation, irritability, and psychomotor slowdown are frequent with growing depression. Sexual interest decreases. As the depression grows, thoughts of a compulsive nature may present themselves, with crying spells, suicidal ideas, and wishes to be free of the "black feeling." The person then is almost unable to function without great

1. Willard Wagner, "The Voices on Psychiatry," in *Hospital Ministry,* ed. Lawrence E. Holst (New York: Crossroad, 1985), p. 153.

difficulty and effort. The isolation from others only adds to the acute pain, and a sudden lag in normal interests may be an attempt to cope with depression.[2]

PASTORAL CARE NEEDED

Support is one of the most helpful ministries a pastor can offer the depressed patient. Other patients with emotional illness may also need help in exploring their inner world in order to make sense out of what seems to be confused and absurd. *Dialogue* provides this kind of help, when pastor and patient join in a mutual exploration of the dynamic meaning at the base of the patient's bizarre feelings and actions. Trust and confidence on an interpersonal level are necessary for this dialogue to be effective. Confidence on the part of the patient may initially come through trust of the pastor's role as pastor. Depressive and other emotionally ill patients often are searching for new meanings to old questions that haunt them. The pastor as teacher can be helpful in clearing up false ideas and distorted theology.

Patients from a rigid religious background usually ask, "Have I committed the unpardonable sin?" Jesus assured the disciples that every sin and blasphemy will be forgiven except blasphemy against the Spirit: "And whoever says a word against the Son of Man will be forgiven; but whoever speaks against the Holy Spirit will not be forgiven, either in this age or in the age to come" (Matt. 12:32).

2. Joe Boone Abbott, "Depressive Reactions and Pastoral Care," in *Pastor and Patient,* ed. Richard Dayringer (New York: Jason Aronson, 1982), pp. 33-34.

Scholars are by no means in agreement on the meaning of this passage. Eduard Schweizer writes that "what is probably meant, then, is that lack of faith is forgivable as long as it is merely a response to a report about the Son of Man, but not when the great works of the Spirit, described in verse 28, take place."[3]

Sherman E. Johnson, quoting B. H. Branscomb, says, "Perhaps the thought is: 'To ascribe the Spirit's work to Satan is to overturn all moral values. He who takes such an attitude shuts himself out from forgiveness by his very stubbornness and impenitence. Words against Jesus are not as serious as those spoken against the Spirit, for they may arise out of misunderstanding.' "[4]

Persons who worry about having committed the unpardonable sin can be told that their faith in God the Father, Son, and Holy Spirit is an assurance that they have not committed this sin. Concern about this sin may be an expression of mental depression, deep-seated guilt, or a feeling of despair, and as these are dealt with by physician and pastor, people may overcome this fear.

Patients with emotional illness may feel that God is punishing them for imagined sins as well as real ones. The pastor can read and interpret Scripture that gives the assurance of forgiveness to those who repent and turn to God and, in addition, can seek to embody the words spoken by demonstrating consistent, steadfast love.

---

3. Edward Schweizer, *The Good News According to Matthew* (Atlanta: John Knox Press, 1977), p. 288.

4. Sherman E. Johnson, "Introduction and Exegesis of St. Matthew," *The Interpreter's Bible*, vol. 7 (Nashville: Abingdon Press, 1979), p. 400.

Some patients become ill because of exposure to a sick religion that emphasizes God's wrath and eternal punishment, with very little said about God's mercy and pardon. Some people are trapped by feelings of resentment toward the church for past hurts. The pastor can help them explore these feelings and begin to see the church as both human and divine.

Willard Wagner points out that at times, supportive ministry is the best kind a pastor can provide. Supportive ministry "employs methods that seek to stabilize, undergird, nurture, motivate, or guide troubled persons, enabling them to handle their problems and relationships more constructively within whatever limits are imposed by their personality resources and circumstances."[5]

The goal of supportive ministry is to help people cope effectively with their present situation by using their inner strengths as well as the outer resources available. It is focused on the here and now. A variety of relationships, both within the hospital and in the patient's network of family and friends, can be drawn on. "To help to restore and strengthen those relationships is a vital goal of supportive ministry. In supportive counseling we 'lend' our ego, our strength, our wisdom to troubled persons in order to help them to better utilize their own resources and regain a sense of equilibrium," says Wagner.[6]

Drawing on the work of psychiatrist Franz Alexander, Wagner summarizes five procedures used in supportive ministry:

5. Wagner, p. 154.
6. Wagner, p. 154.

1. Emotional Catharsis. Allowing the troubled person to pour out his or her feelings to another who listens and seeks to understand. Not only does this provide emotional relief but it allows that person to overcome loneliness by sharing the burden.

2. Gratify Dependency Needs. The pastor becomes a "good parent," upon whom the person can lean. As any "good parent" the counselor will guide, instruct, and set proper limits and in so doing the patient will be temporarily relieved of the full responsibility for responding to life.

3. Aid the Ego Defenses. Instead of probing or confronting, instead of challenging defenses, the counselor will support those defenses which are enabling the person to hold together during the crisis.

4. Objective View of the Stress Situation. An important aspect of supportive ministry is to provide an objective overview of the immediate crisis. This enables the person to more realistically explore alternative options and to make appropriate decisions.

5. Modifying the Life Situation. On occasion it becomes necessary to change the environment or to remove the person from the environment so that he or she has a better chance to recover personal strengths and resources. In a sense, a psychiatric hospitalization is an environmental manipulation intended to temporarily remove one from the stresses and burdens of one's life.[7]

A supportive ministry is *compassionate,* which means "suffering with another." Pastors will need to be aware of

7. Wagner, p. 154.

their own anxiety in offering a supportive ministry. There may be a temptation to do or say something to take away the patient's pain. "Supportive ministry is often patient, quiet listening, allowing the patient's own resources and strength to emerge," says Wagner.[8]

The very heart of ministry to the emotionally ill consists of enabling the patient to hear and experience God's forgiveness through Scripture, prayer, and relationships. Forgiveness is to the religious dimension of life what medicine is to the physical. Through witnessing to the power of the living Christ to remake the patient's life, a pastor may be able to help the patient find new hope and a new beginning. The root of depression for some patients has been found to be the need for rebirth, not as a theological concept, but as a shared experience.

PRAYER

O God, we praise and adore you. You have made us for yourself, and without you we can find no rest or peace for our souls. We confess our weakness of faith and trust in you. We worry about the future and what is going to happen to us and to those we love. We fear the worst, and sometimes we feel all hope is lost. Heavenly Father, we pray for N., asking that your peace which passes all understanding may be in and with *(him/her)*. May N. know that your everlasting arms are underneath and around *(him/her)*. Reassure us that nothing can separate us from your love in Christ Jesus our Lord. We thank you for the assurance Jesus gives us: "Peace I leave with you; my peace I give to you. I do not

8. Wagner, p. 155.

give to you as the world gives. Do not let your hearts be troubled, and do not let them be afraid" (John 14:27). God, grant us the serenity to accept the things we cannot change, enable us to change the things we can, and give us wisdom to know the difference. We pray in Christ's name. Amen.

Scripture

- Job 19:23-27
- Job 42:1-6
- Psalm 22:1-5, 14-15, 19, 22-24
- Psalm 23 (p. 171 below)
- Psalm 51:1-17
- Psalm 118: 1-9
- Proverbs 17:22 (p. 173 below)
- Isaiah 35:1-10
- Isaiah 40:28-31 (p. 173 below)
- Isaiah 55:10-13 (p. 174 below)
- Jeremiah 17:7-8, 14 (p. 174 below)
- John 3:16-18 (p. 177 below)
- Romans 5:1-5 (p. 178 below)
- Romans 8:31-39 (p. 179 below)
- 1 John 1:5-9
- 1 Peter 6:6-9

12

GASTROINTESTINAL ILLNESSES

Perhaps no illness links emotions and body more than does that associated with gastrointestinal (GI) problems. Bodily functions may be grouped as they relate to taking in, retaining, and eliminating. *Taking in* is the function of the mouth, stomach, and upper end of the GI tract. At that end of the tract, peptic ulcers occur. Robert B. Lantz points out that "one outstanding symptom of a peptic ulcer is what the patient often calls 'hunger pains.' He/she strives to satisfy these pains by taking in, whether it be food or responsibility, attention or love. This, however, only heightens his/her frustration and his/her symptoms."[1]

Ulcerative colitis occurs at the other end of the GI tract — the section where *retaining and eliminating* occur. Patients with ailments in this area often are unable to return or retain affection, says Lantz.

At the time of this writing a peptic ulcer is considered a chronic disease. It cannot be cured but can be controlled by proper diet and medical care. Emotional factors are definitely involved, in addition to certain foods and

1. Robert B. Lantz, "Care of the Patient with Gastrointestinal Complaints," in *Pastor and Patient,* ed. Richard Dayringer (New York: Jason Aronson, 1982), p. 142.

chemicals. A pastor will want to work with the physician and psychiatrist (if involved) in shaping pastoral care, and will also want to read the best recent literature on the subject. Social adjustment may be an aspect of the treatment program, and here you can be of help as patients reevaluate their relationships with others.

Ulcerative colitis also is chronic and intermittent. Persons likely to suffer from this illness are generally anxious and eager to please but have difficulty establishing a close relationship with other people. They repress their emotions and seldom if ever express feelings of hostility. "Emotion-laden situations such as sickness, death, bereavement, loss of money, as well as other precipitating factors, may bring about an aggravation of the illness," writes Lantz, who observes further that "it has also been found that it breaks out after verbal humiliation in the presence of others, or the traumatic loss of a dependent person."[2] The parent-child relationship factor in this illness usually involves a mother who is possessive and overprotective and a father who is often domineering and aggressive. While regulation and diet are used in treatment, the main factor in alleviating a patient's symptoms is a constructive relationship.

PASTORAL CARE NEEDED

Be concerned about the *past* history of these patients and the role of forgiveness and reconciliation in gaining health. Frequent visits — daily when possible — and pastoral counseling for a few weeks to several months may

2. Lantz, p. 144.

be called for. "The focus of the visits would tend toward relating the patient's past relationships and experiences to their current and expected equivalents. . . . It is important that the minister offer a relationship which though authoritative by nature of the pastoral office, is nevertheless warm and symbolic of God's eternal understanding of man's soulful struggles," advocates Lantz. Get to know the patient's socioeconomic background and career ambitions. These disorders are most prevalent in "the more fluid upward-moving groups, [therefore] it becomes . . . important to relate the socioeconomic struggles with the patient's concept of himself and his relationship to those persons significant in his life."[3] The pastor can be of great help to these patients in working through their emotions and developing more positive, healthy relationships.

Since this illness has definite emotional factors, humor can be a means of helping the patient live with what may be a chronic condition. Humor may help the patient deal with relationships and put himself or herself in proper perspective.

PRAYER

O God, you have created us in your image and for relationship with you, and we confess our need for you in the center of our lives. You have made us for yourself, and our souls are restless until they rest in you. Help us to heal our memories of the past by the power of your Spirit. Let us put our trust in you as our Rock, our Redeemer, and our ultimate security. Take away our worry and frustra-

3. Lantz, p. 147.

tion. May we find peace, love, and security in relationship with you — now and in the days ahead. We pray for the health-care team as they care for *N*. May we know your presence in a new and more real way, now and in the weeks and months ahead. Amen.

Scripture

- Psalm 18, selected verses
- Psalm 23 (p. 171 below)
- Psalm 34
- Psalm 103
- Proverbs 17:22 (p. 173 below)
- Matthew 5:1-12
- Romans 5:1-5 (p. 178 below)
- Romans 8:31-39 (p. 179 below)

13

INTENSIVE CARE PATIENTS

The Intensive Care Unit (ICU) is a fairly recent innovation, but its use is expanding. The patient, family, nursing personnel, and medical staff all need the pastor's understanding and strengthening ministry. Family members are often anxious, even to the point of being distraught, but still they hope for recovery of the patient. The usual concerns become magnified under the unfamiliar stresses; the strange sights, sounds, and smells may increase the anxiety and trauma already being experienced by the patient. "Death anxiety, generalized apprehension, boredom, loneliness, guilt, denial of the reality of their condition, irritability, depression, despair, and resentment are all a part of the negativities which are experienced by ICU patients," writes David M. Hurst.[1]

PASTORAL CARE NEEDED

In caring for ICU patients, pastors should engage in self-examination to discover those attitudes and perspectives that make for wholeness in their own spiritual makeup. This

1. David M. Hurst, "Pastoral Care in the Intensive Care Unit," in *Pastor and Patient,* ed. Richard Dayringer (New York: Jason Aronson, 1982), p. 150.

includes the resolution of feelings about their own death and feelings of insecurity, and their reliance upon experiential faith and hope. In addition, they will want to help a patient examine and reaffirm faith in God, hope for the future, and love for God, family, friends, and others.

Caution should be used in employing humor with the ICU patient. Humor may be the appropriate tool for communicating care and support, but this must be carefully weighed for each patient.

There are two principal phases in ministry to ICU patients, based on a patient's condition. The critically ill, sedated, very weak patient may respond more to nonverbal communication, expressed in the pastor's role as God's minister. Convalescing patients may find a verbal, friendly relationship more helpful. These patients, feeling stronger, more alert, and well-oriented, will crave companionship and conversation.

Identify yourself clearly to the person who admits visitors. By requesting permission, a pastor is allowed to visit at times other than those permitted to the family. A brief visit of a very few minutes is usually preferable. A visit of more than five to seven minutes puts a strain on the patient and may interfere with the work of the health-care team. A pastor's affirmation of the nursing staff, expressing thanks for their care and including them in prayers with and for the patient, will be supportive of people in high-stress work.

Hurst offers the following practical suggestions and warnings for pastoral care in the ICU:

1. The minister should learn from the chaplain or other health-care team member what to expect in the

ICU so that he or she will experience a minimum of shock, anxiety, or revulsion over what is seen, heard, and smelled there.

2. It is advisable to always check with the charge nurse to learn something of each patient's condition before visiting.

3. The pastor should approach the patient with an attitude of controlled confidence, hope, and expectancy.

4. The pastor's voice should be kept low and an unhurried manner should be followed in order to communicate a soothing and strengthening influence as the pastor offers himself or herself to help make the patient's burden more bearable.

5. If the patient's eyes are closed, or the patient is comatose or does not recognize the pastor, then the pastor should identify himself or herself immediately to let the patient know who is visiting.

6. Visits should be kept brief but as frequent as seems appropriate and permitted by the pastor's schedule.

7. The pastor should use his or her informed intuition and skills in pastoral care in supporting the patient, the patient's relatives, and the health-care team during this very stressful time.[2]

Prayer

O God, our help in ages past, our hope for years to come, be present with us now in this time of special need. We acknowledge you as our Creator and Redeemer, our Rock

2. Hurst, pp. 155-56.

in time of distress. We pray for your servant *N.,* asking your healing power to work in *(his/her)* life. Grant that your Spirit may strengthen the inner person and give courage, faith, and hope. We thank you for the doctors and nurses who are caring for *N.* Give them divine wisdom and healing power, we pray. Be near to *N.*'s family and friends as they wait and pray for healing. We confess our faith in you and trust your promise to be with us always. Through Christ our Lord we pray. Amen.

Scripture

- Psalm 23 (p. 171 below)
- Psalm 139, selected verses
- Isaiah 40:28-31 (p. 173 below)
- Isaiah 43:1*b*-2, 5*a*
- Romans 8:26-27 (p. 178 below)
- Romans 8:31-39 (p. 179 below)

14

THE KIDNEY PATIENT

A patient with kidney failure may be either on kidney dialysis or preparing for or undergoing a kidney transplant. Persons with kidney failure may deny that they are sick, which is an emotional defense. In the initial period, when a parishioner first learns of kidney failure, seek to build a firm relationship in order to be of help later when the patient's body chemistry makes things much more difficult. Listen to the person's life story, noting the "stepping stones" and previous crises.

When the renal function begins to affect eating and sleeping patterns and sexual activity, the person may become depressed and irritable. A marked change in personality may occur; the person may become quite paranoid or obsessive-compulsive. As the illness intensifies, the patient may respond to the pastor in a disinterested manner. Anger may be expressed, with complaints against hospital staff or things in general. Later the person may feel guilty for expressing anger or may doubt the care physicians are giving. The patient may cheat on the prescribed diet or, if still working, may take on extra work. The classic questions may be asked: Why is God doing this to me? What have I done to deserve this illness and suffering?

The family will become anxious and bewildered at the radical change in personality and conduct. The equilibrium of the family system will be upset, and if the patient is married, sexual relations will be impaired. And there may be financial problems resulting from the illness.

There are three choices for the patient with kidney failure: (1) Do nothing, which leads to death, (2) go on a dialysis machine, or (3) receive a kidney transplant.

PASTORAL CARE NEEDED

You can play a vital role in working with the family, especially as facilitator. Help family members understand what is happening in the patient's body and personality, and in their relationships with the patient. It is important to listen as they share their hurt, anger, bewilderment.

Help the patient make the best decision by listening and reflecting what he or she is feeling. Denial may be a useful defense for the patient, and when strong it should be left alone, but it can be counterproductive. Call on the hospital chaplain, when available, to work in a consultative relationship, but of course this action would not relieve you of responsibility for pastoral care.

Patients on a dialysis machine may feel dependent and have ambivalent feelings about living or dying. They may complain and feel depersonalized in depending on a machine for life. Or the illness may cause patients to say they have lost faith in God, or that God is dead or absent. A "lament" from Scripture may help patients realize that others have cried out against God, who seemed unconcerned or absent, yet those others have worked through the crisis to faith. When a kidney must be transplanted, allow the patient to ventilate feelings of doubt, anger, and frustration in daily affairs.

If a new kidney works well, there is cause for thanksgiving and celebration. Recovering patients may want to reorder their lives as a result of this miracle of modern medicine. Especially when younger, they may want to dedicate their lives to service to others out of a sense of being indebted for this gift of life. The recovering transplant patient may want to be left alone for the first six to nine months, and the minister can help in interpersonal relations during this time. Be sure everyone understands that although the kidney is functioning, the patient is not fully recovered and will *never* be the same as before the operation.

Humor with the kidney patient may help the patient affirm living and deal with depression. It should be carefully chosen humor.

It is a unique function of the pastor, as a member of the health-care team working with a kidney patient, to see the patient in the *family system*, to work with all members of the family.

Prayer

O God, our help in ages past, our hope for years to come, we come to you with a special concern for N. We acknowledge that you are the Lord of life and that Jesus is the divine Physician. We pray for wisdom as N. makes a difficult decision which will affect not only *(his/her)* own life but that of those around *(him/her)*. We pray for guidance for the health-care team as its members care for N. We pray for your Spirit to come anew upon N. to heal and give courage, faith, and hope. May *N.* know that you are always near, and underneath are the everlasting arms. Enable *N.* to change those things that can be changed, to accept those things that cannot be changed, and to have the wisdom to know the difference. We pray through Christ our Lord. Amen.

Scripture

- Psalm 23 (p. 171 below)
- Psalm 42
- Psalm 139
- Isaiah 40:28-31 (p. 173 below)

15

OBSTETRICS

One woman told her minister that when her first child was born she received much attention because of complications and the premature child's tenuous hold on life. But when her second child was born quite normally, she received little attention. Pregnancy and childbirth can be a time of either joy or loneliness.

My own parents knew deep sorrow when their first child died within a few hours of birth. They had married later in life, and the death was a source of great disappointment and grief. A few years later another child was born, followed in two years by yet another. But in a little cemetery in Cuba, Alabama, lies the child none of us knew but all mourned.

The time of pregnancy and birth is a deeply spiritual time for many couples. Some may see their child as their own creation, a possession to be nurtured for their own enjoyment. Others, filled with awe and wonder, see their child as a gift from God, loaned to them and entrusted to their care.

Susan Johnson Kline writes that "the birth of a baby can elicit other spiritual attitudes. A child can be seen by either father or mother as a competitor for a limited quantity of love; as a threat to a new parent's sense of competency; or as the fulfillment of a partnership, the very purpose for which a couple was married."[1] Kline calls attention to the great emphasis placed in the last ten years by pastors, physicians, and ethicists upon the dramatic obstetrical issues: stillbirths, high-risk infants, cessation-of-treatment questions, elective and therapeutic abortions, amniocentesis, and genetic counseling.

In recent years there has been a shift in the context of childbirth and related ministries from the earlier anesthetized and isolating experience to an alert and active participation. We have moved through a phase when childbirth was seen as involving only a woman to one in which both parents participate as partners. It is now a drama among partners: mother and child, childbirth coach (usually the father) and mother, doctors and parents, and even grandparents. The woman is more often a full partner in the marriage, earning a share of the income, and the parents share in child raising.

Kline points up this shift — from a theology that "focused primarily on a masculine God who created man and woman 'to be fruitful and multiply' (the woman 'to have pain in childbearing') to a God with whom we are in responsible partnership as co-creators, and in whom we can recognize both masculine and feminine faces." We now view God as one who participates in the whole journey of our lives, from birth to death. This affirmation of the equal partnership of men and women in parenting "is revealing of a greater understanding of God's nature," says Kline.[2]

1. Susan Johnson Kline, "The Voices on Obstetrics," in *Hospital Ministry,* ed. Lawrence E. Holst (New York: Crossroad, 1985), p. 79.
2. Kline, p. 81.

Pastoral Care Needed

While there is great joy over the birth of a healthy child, there is deep sorrow when a baby is stillborn or dies soon after birth. Parents cry, "What kind of God would let this happen?" Many questions of theodicy are raised as the parents ask why an all-good, all-powerful God would allow their child to die. Kline observes that "whereas pregnancy and the birth of a baby can awaken a sense of innocence in adults, it can also tap into a deep knowledge of their vulnerability to loss. . . . When a baby is born with problems, parents realize that life is not fair and rage against it. They will never be so innocent again."[3] The Society of Compassionate Friends offers supportive friendship to grieving parents. Membership is composed of parents who have experienced the death of a child.

A child born with some deformity or mental deficiency may cause mixed feelings in parents — feelings of joy that the child is born, but disappointment and fear for the child's future adjustment.

The experience of childbirth puts many mothers in touch with the mystery of God's creation and can be the time when they feel closest to God. The pastor can build upon those feelings and the mystery and awe of childbirth. A hymn such as "Now Thank We All Our God" or a psalm of celebration and gratitude may express these feelings. If possible, see the baby during your visit and join with mother and father in celebrating the arrival of the child. First-time parents are especially joyful, but they also feel a new sense of responsibility for the newborn child.

3. Kline, p. 87.

Humor may help add to the joy of welcoming a healthy infant, but would not be appropriate for other births.

Kline, both a chaplain and a mother, says she sees her role as participant and partner with parents, demonstrating "a model of God's relationship with them, and their relationship with one another. . . . I do see birth as being a private event, as well as one in which there is a great deal of public interest. My participation is offered with the aim of 'making space' for the parent's own needs."[4] In ministering to parents of both normal and abnormal deliveries, Kline has developed three working assumptions:

1. *Whatever is occurring is a family-centered experience, and affects both partners (whether married or not), as well as grandparents and siblings. . . .* In the case of an infant death, this assumption makes me respectful of the father's as well as mother's style of grieving. Frequently a father becomes fiercely protective, deciding for his wife whether she should see or hold their dead baby. In those cases, I attempt to respond to his grief, rather than immediately assume an advocacy role for the mother. I also am sensitive to the double grief which grandparents experience in a birth crisis; they not only are sad for the illness or death of their grandchild, but also feel helpless to comfort their own child.

2. *It is important to allow parents to be confronted with the reality of their situation, rather than protected from it.* This applies more to crisis ministry than to normal pregnancies. . . . Whenever anything challenges the parents' fantasy, it constitutes a crisis for the

4. Kline, p. 89.

parents. Their "crushed dreams" may be as simple as a baby of the opposite gender from their expectations. Or it may be as devastating as a stillbirth or baby with gross anomalies which will allow for survival, but for a very changed child-parent relationship. . . . Parents have confirmed that it is extremely important that they be offered the opportunity to see their baby, no matter how small. Fantasies about its appearance are usually worse than the reality.

3. *It is important to create positive memories while parents are [in the hospital], because, for many, these are their only memories of their child outside the womb.*[5]

Kline tells of baptizing stillborn infants. Pastors will want to think through their theology of baptism and be prepared to respond appropriately. Protestant theology in this regard differs rather widely from Roman Catholic theology. For a more appropriate response, in light of some traditions, offer a prayer and read appropriate Scripture with the parent or parents.

The prayer would express grief, lack of understanding as to "why" the child did not live, and trust in God in the face of death. Pastors are cautioned against praying or making statements to the effect that "God in his infinite wisdom" took the child, or "God needed another flower in heaven," or "God needed the infant in heaven more than we do on earth." Be careful not to blame God for what is mysterious or results from natural causes. The prayer should emphasize God's abiding love and care for the stillborn child and for the parents and family.

5. Kline, pp. 89-90.

Prayer (for a normal-delivery baby)

O God, who has created us to celebrate life, we pause to give thanks for the safe arrival of N. We thank you for *(mother's name)* and her safe delivery. Grant her strength in the days ahead as she and *(father's name)* care for their new child. We thank you for the physicians, nurses, and others on the health-care team. We feel your presence in a very special way in these moments of joy and celebration for N.'s healthy arrival. Be with *(her/his)* parents as they care for *(her/him)*, and guide *(her/him)* all the days of *(her/his)* life by the power of your Spirit. Through Christ we pray. Amen.

Scripture

- Psalm 100 (p. 172 below)
- Psalm 139:1-14, 23-24
- Ecclesiastes 3:1-8
- Ecclesiastes 11:5
- Isaiah 40:28-31 (p. 173 below)
- Luke 18:15-17 (p. 177 below)
- Philippians 4:1, 4-7 (p. 181 below)

16

THE PRESURGICAL PATIENT

Anxiety is the major reaction of most people to surgery. The patient experiences anxiety, and family and friends also experience anxiety, which aggravates the patient's inner stress. The major cause of presurgical anxiety is the possibility of acute pain, radical body damage, or death. Fear of the unknown, coupled with fear of the outcome, also plays a large part.

Appropriate humor can help presurgical patients deal with anxiety and inner stress. It should be carefully used, however, so that the patient and family do not feel that the minister is being flippant about the operation.

Studies reveal that persons with religious faith are less anxious than those with no religious preference. Children and people over sixty years of age seem to be less anxious, and women generally are more anxious than men.

Pastoral Care Needed

The pastor can be of great help to patients by listening and helping them verbalize their fears. Often a patient only wants a caring person with whom to share fears; fear often is less intense when shared. Do not attempt to minimize these fears, but explore with the patient the depths of the anxiety.

In addition to listening, communicate God's abiding love and continuing mercy, assuring the patient that God never fails or forsakes, but is "as near as hands or feet, or breathing itself." The sacraments may be offered as they seem appropriate.

If surgery has been cancelled or rescheduled, the patient may be depressed or hostile, or both. Find out why the surgery was cancelled or rescheduled. Was the surgeon ill or called out of town? Did tests reveal something new? The patient always wants to know and often imagines that things are worse than they are. Thus discovery of the reason for cancellation or rescheduling may be useful in shaping the pastoral visit. The ventilation of these feelings with the pastor can be helpful.

A pastoral visit the night *before* surgery may be very comforting for both patient and family. When a visit in person is not possible, a telephone call and prayer by phone can be supportive. If you plan to be present for the surgery, it is wise to arrive *before* the patient is medicated, which may take place an hour or so before the operation is scheduled. Operations are sometimes rescheduled for later in the day or earlier than planned. It is helpful to check with the charge nurse about the time to make this visit.

Prayer with the patient, family, friends, and health-care personnel just before the patient is taken from the room is recommended. Those present may join hands around the bed for this prayer in a symbolic affirmation of unity.

Studies indicate that patients who will undergo surgery, like other people under intense stress, are more open to help. The minister intervenes in the crisis as one who is more calm and stable, one who assures the person that his or her feelings are acceptable and that the crisis can be resolved. Patients who have adequate support and information about what to expect feel less pain, recover more quickly, and are released earlier.

Prayer

Our heavenly Father, we come to you, our Rock and Salvation, asking for your peace. You wait upon us when we are restless. You give us courage when we are anxious. Now in the quietness of this time, grant us confidence that you are with us in this hour and in the days ahead. We pray for those who will operate and assist. Grant them wisdom and divine healing power. We commit ourselves to your keeping, as we pray in Jesus' name. Amen.

Scripture

- Psalm 14
- Psalm 18
- Psalm 23 (p. 171 below)
- Psalm 90:1-2
- Psalm 121 (p. 172 below)
- Philippians 4:1, 4-7 (p. 181 below)
- Hebrews 11:1-3, 8-12 (p. 182 below)

17

THE STROKE PATIENT

A stroke is a cerebral vascular accident (CVA) which involves the delicate brain tissues that govern the bodily
functions. A stroke has been called a physical, intellectual,
and emotional vortex. Webster defines this type of vortex
as "a region within the body of fluid in which the fluid
elements have an angular velocity; something that re-
sembles a whirlpool." The effect of a stroke may range
from no change in the state of consciousness to sudden
death or coma. Physical damage may result in mild numb-
ness of a limb or other part of the body or extensive
paralysis and dysfunction requiring physical therapy;
there may be paralysis of one side of the face and speech
difficulties; the mind may be slightly confused, or a radical
change in personality may result. Most patients can make
some progress, however, and helpful information is available from the National Stroke Association, Inc., 7330
Greenville Ave., Dallas, TX 75231; Tel. 1-800-527-6941.

A stroke usually produces physical and emotional regression manifested in self-centeredness. A brief attention
span and difficulty with abstract thinking may result,
though depression and the related emotion, anger, are
dominant characteristics. Patients who are depressed will
experience a conflict between fear of dying and fear of
living, a feeling of hopelessness. They may cry or laugh at

inappropriate times and therefore tend to withdraw from social contact. They may lash out both physically and verbally — against God, family, health-care team, and pastor. While they may be uncooperative and express the wish to be left alone, suicide rarely occurs.

Rudolph E. Grantham sums up the effects of a stroke: "Breakdown in communication and physical ability in the form of paralysis, regression, depression, and anger stand out as central factors in our understanding strokes as 'physical and intellectual impairment.'"[1] Patients may recall early life experiences easily but be unable to remember recent events. They may long for their mother and other early childhood security sources such as touching, soothing sounds, and so on. Patients are aware of being adults but are unable to care for themselves; emotional discomfort is increased by this conflict between adulthood and enforced regression.

PASTORAL CARE NEEDED

The first objective is to reestablish communication, which may be difficult if there has been major brain damage. A patient may even be in a state of impaired consciousness: lethargy; obtundation, a state of dull indifference; stupor, from which a person can be aroused only by vigorous stimulation; moderate coma, in which only rudimentary motor responses occur; or deep coma, in which psychological and motor responses to stimulation are lost. Talk with

---

1. Rudolph E. Grantham, "Pastoral Care of the Stroke Patient," in *Pastor and Patient,* ed. Richard Dayringer (New York: Jason Aronson, 1982), p. 170.

the physician or head nurse about the physical and emotional state of the patient to determine if it is in the best interest of the patient to try to communicate at that time.

Grantham advises that communication with the stroke patient should be *brief and simple.* Speak clearly and slowly, extending a message of comfort, help, and perhaps challenge. A touch may convey the message of love and concern and break through the patient's isolation more effectively than words. Grantham writes:

> Sometimes the unconscious patient will respond to hymns and memorized Bible verses, such as the Twenty-third Psalm and Aaron's benediction (Num. 6:23-26). Where worship has been a meaningful part of the person's life, it may be the means whereby the will to live is strengthened. Often the severely ill person who is unable to receive verbal communication will respond to personally meaningful religious symbols. . . . The minister offers not only his love and services, he also symbolizes God's love for the patient.[2]

A pastor's own emotional state is critical in working with a stroke patient. If you are disturbed, repulsed, or uneasy, this will be communicated nonverbally. At this point, seek to convey *agape,* unconditional love, and a warm regard for the patient. Faith is a key factor in ministry to the stroke patient — faith in God's goodness, faith in the patient's power to heal, faith in the health-care team. Show sensitive understanding and be willing to take the initiative in conversation.

2. Grantham, p. 171.

Humor may be an appropriate means of communicating with the stroke patient and a way of expressing care.

In addition to supportive counseling, concentrate on strengthening the patient's will to live. Stroke patients need to find a valid purpose for living in their new condition. The "Serenity Prayer" of Reinhold Niebuhr (see p. 166 below) may assist them to accept their limitations. The pastor may need to help patients stop straining and pushing ahead and wait upon God, as receptive vessels.

Grief therapy also strengthens the will to live by encouraging patients to talk about the significant persons or things they may have lost — body image, purpose, work, and so on.

Some stroke patients die, but we can help them die with dignity. Physicians report that most are in a coma when death comes, and since this limits ministry to the patient, more care should be directed toward the family.

The pastor also can minister to the patient *through* the family. There is psychological unity between husband and wife, and a stroke in one can be devastating to the other. The family may experience physical and emotional exhaustion, fear, pregrief, guilt, and disrupted work and daily life, plus financial problems. A supportive and educative ministry is needed. The pastor may advise the family to help the patient by *avoiding* yielding to the person's dependency.

In summary, make verbal or nonverbal contact, provide support to patient and family, and work to increase the patient's will to live.

Prayer

Heavenly Father, we your children turn to you because we know you are already present with us through your Spirit. Even when we cannot speak, we know your Spirit helps us in our weakness. We do not know how to pray as we should, but your Spirit intercedes for us with sighs too deep for words. We thank you for your Spirit, who intercedes for us according to your will. We pray for *N.* Be especially near to *(him/her)* and guide the doctors and other members of the health-care team who care for *(him/her)*. We pray for healing for *N.* Encourage us with hope and faith, we pray.

Strengthen and uphold *(his/her)* family, and especially be with *(care-giver)* as *(he/she)* cares for *N.* We know you are near, even when you seem absent. We thank you that nothing can separate us from your love in Christ Jesus our Lord. Through Christ we pray. Amen.

Scripture

- Exodus 33:14-15
- Deuteronomy 33:27 (p. 171 below)
- Psalm 23 (p. 171 below)
- Psalm 46
- Isaiah 41:10
- Romans 8:31-39 (p. 179 below)
- 1 Peter 6:6-9

18

THE SUBSTANCE ABUSE PATIENT

Almost an equal number of men and women are alcoholics, and the primary abusers are middle-aged people. Since it is estimated that there are ten alcoholics for every addict or abuser of all other drugs, we must consider alcohol along with other drugs in a chemical package. One listing shows types of drugs in order of dependence: (1) alcohol, (2) depressant and stimulant pills, (3) hallucinogens, and (4) narcotics.

Several warning signs of progressive alcohol or drug dependence can appear: preoccupation, rapid use, hiding, solitary use, tolerance, unpredictability, memory blackout, and universality.[1] Most people try to hide their addiction at school or at work, but when problems appear there, the illness usually is present. More often now, employers are giving drug-dependent employees a choice: get treatment or get fired.

Anderson emphasizes that "the most effective intervention in most situations of alcoholism or other drug dependence is *to help the family free itself from feeling trapped*

---

1. Carl Anderson, "The Voices of Substance Abuse," in *Hospital Ministry,* ed. Lawrence E. Holst (New York: Crossroad, 1985), pp. 166-67.

by the illness and to begin making positive changes in its own response to the illness."[2] Change is more likely to occur when a family firmly begins a new behavior pattern in its relation with the addict. A more realistic situation is created as the addict is no longer shielded and the consequences of the sick behavior are no longer removed.

"Never let an addict off the hook of responsibility for the immorality of his abusive chemicals or concomitantly immoral life. Alcoholics Anonymous zeroes in on guilt with two painfully marvelous steps from their Twelve Step program," emphasizes E. W. Belter.[3] In Steps 4 and 5, addicts are asked to take a morally searching inventory of their lives and to admit to God, self, and another human being the exact nature of their shortcomings. Notice that this inventory is not primarily concerned with chemical abuse, but with the addictions of each of us — self-centeredness, greed, lust, envy, prejudice, pride, phoniness — sins that result from our rebellion against God.

PASTORAL CARE NEEDED

Addicts and abusers need assurance of believable grace, the atoning work of Christ. All humans find the feeling of rejection and unworthiness unbearable. Everyone needs relief from guilt. The pastor can bear witness to the love and forgiveness of God in spite of our unworthiness.

---

2. Anderson, p. 168.

3. E. W. Belter, "Ministering to Persons with Drug Dependency Problems," in *Pastor and Patient,* ed. Richard Dayringer (New York: Jason Aronson, 1982), p. 114.

Families, employers, and associates need to be involved as part of a patient's treatment team. Belter says, "But let us first and foremost deal with his relationship to Christ. . . . We must bring him to face guilt; to hear the gospel, the good news of God's love and grace; to surrender to Christ's forgiveness; and to know the power of the Holy Spirit for rebirth each day."[4]

Of all the patients, the recovering alcoholic and drug addict may have the best sense of humor as they reflect on what their addictions did to them and the funny things they did as addicts. Humor is one way of responding to God's forgiveness and expressing joy over freedom from bondage to addictions.

Investigate treatment centers in your area and be prepared to recommend one, in consultation with an addict's physician. A get-acquainted visit to a center can be very helpful later.

PRAYER

Our loving and gracious God, we praise and adore you. We come to you as sinners saved by grace, acknowledging our need for forgiveness. We pray for N., asking for courage to get help in dealing with chemical abuse. We pray for *(his/her)* family and friends as they offer support and express concern for N.'s health and happiness. Pour out your Spirit upon N.'s life and give healing and strength to the inner being. We pray through Christ, who died that we might have life and have it abundantly. Amen.

4. Belter, p. 117.

Scripture

- Psalm 23 (p. 171 below)
- Isaiah 1:18
- Isaiah 43:1*b*-2, 5*a*
- Romans 5:1-5 (p. 178 below)
- 1 Peter 6:6-9

19

THE SURGICAL PATIENT

In an earlier chapter we dealt with anxiety and other issues of presurgical patients; this chapter deals with surgical patients and their families. While some surgery is elective and routine, most involves risk and stress for both patient and family. In fact, many times the family is in greater need of ministry than is the patient.

John Florell has described a process of crisis intervention that has proven effective. He urges that "giving the patients a reference point, helping them focus on the experience of surgery, aiding them in making sense out of the whole experience of surgery and recovery through information, and letting the patients know they were cared for has a significant impact on the healing process." A study indicates that patients given information and emotional support experience less pain, recover more quickly, and are able to be released earlier.[1]

Patients usually are moved from surgery to a recovery room where vital signs are monitored and medication is given. Some patients then go to a less intensive care unit, while others go to intensive care for a period of time before

1. John Florell, "Crisis Intervention in Orthopedic Surgery," in *Pastor and Patient,* ed. Richard Dayringer (New York: Jason Aronson, 1982), p. 95.

returning to their own rooms. Important crisis ministry also takes place in the lounge where relatives and friends wait. This is a very stressful time.

Pastoral Care Needed

Going into the hospital for surgery has different meanings for different patients, but almost all have some feeling of apprehension. The underlying emotion is fear. Surgical patients who have reflected on the experience "describe it as a fear of nonbeing, a fear of death. They are afraid they won't make it. They focus on fear of the anesthesia, which seems to be a symbol of nonbeing, of going into the uttermost depths of the unknown from which they may never again emerge," writes Marion Kanaly. Kanaly emphasizes that "being (or feeling) out of control is a corollary dynamic of the basic fear and anxiety that surgical patients experience."[2]

In addition, "*The person going to surgery knows that life itself is about to be managed and ordered totally by others for a period of time. Here is the ultimate and absolute loss of control over oneself.* Heartbeat and breath will be maintained through the direction of other people, not the I who hitherto has been in charge."[3]

Some patients manage this loss of control very well, while others become excessively dependent. Be alert for irritability, resistance, or hostility. Emphasize through conversation, Scripture, and prayer the security we have

2. Marion Kanaly, "The Voices on a Surgical Unit," in *Hospital Ministry,* ed. Lawrence E. Holst (New York: Crossroad, 1985), p. 111.
3. Kanaly, p. 112.

in God, who *is* in ultimate control of our lives, and nurture faith in God's providential care.

Pastors should be aware of their own reactions to a surgical patient's negative feelings. Faithful and skillful pastoral care should be given to those with negative feelings as well as to the cheerful patients with whom we feel more comfortable.

Because patients may not be understood by those caring for them, they may be stereotyped as quiet or as talkative. A quiet person may be left alone and therefore "cut off from needed support," thus increasing the "sense of existential loneliness," the feeling of being an "island unto oneself." Kanaly describes this kind of patient:

> The surgical patient confronts existential loneliness in a real way. *It is the patient who goes alone into the experience.* There are many other people around, but for all their care and help and encouragement, it is the patient who alone submits to the surgeon's scalpel. That is a very lonely place to be. Reflecting postoperatively on the experience, one woman told me: "When they came to wheel me into the operating room and I said goodbye to my husband and daughter, I couldn't stop thinking that this must be what dying is like. You're so alone. No one can do it for you. No one can go through it with you, not really."[4]

Loss of mobility, though usually temporary, is difficult for some patients to cope with.

Through the use of appropriate humor the pastor may

4. Kanaly, p. 113.

141

communicate care and support for the surgical patient. Such humor with patient and family can help ease anxiety and strengthen the sense of community with those present.

A surgical patient needs not only a caring relationship with the pastor but also the assurance of an empathetic community which supports the patient in the special kind of caring Christian community called koinonia. Cards, notes, flowers, and other remembrances mean much to a patient both before and after surgery. The knowledge that individuals of the congregation are praying and that prayers for healing are being offered in corporate worship is supportive and comforting. Some patients may appreciate listening to a cassette recording of the congregation's worship service, to inspirational music, or to Scripture. Favorite television programs may help patients keep in touch with stories and characters, to give continuity and joy to life.

With the pastor's supportive caring ministry, a patient may be able to discover, beyond the pain and emotional stress associated with surgery, a sense of hope and promise, and may feel God's presence in a more real and comforting way.

Prayer

O Divine Physician, we thank you that *N.*'s operation is completed and that *(he/she)* is being supported with prayers, love, and remembrances from family and friends. We thank you for the surgeons and other members of the health-care team. Be especially near to *N.* in these days of recovery. May your Spirit be with *(him/her)* to reassure that *(he/she)* is not alone, but you are always near. We know that although we may feel all alone at times, you are nearer to us than hands or feet or breathing itself. May *N.* find you closer during this time of confinement and pain than ever before. Grant *(him/her)* hope and joy, now and in the days ahead. We pray in Christ's name. Amen.

Scripture

- Psalm 23 (p. 171 below)
- Psalm 103, selected verses
- Psalm 121 (p. 172 below)
- Isaiah 35:1-10
- Matthew 4:23-25
- Mark 2:1-5, 11-12 (p. 176 below)
- Luke 11:9-10 (p. 177 below)
- Romans 5:1-5 (p. 178 below)
- 2 Corinthians 4:7-9 (p. 180 below)
- Philippians 4:1, 4-7 (p. 181 below)

20

THE UNCONSCIOUS PATIENT

Rather than thinking of patients as either conscious or un-conscious, we should think of stages of recovery, from un-consciousness to consciousness. Thus on a scale of 1 to 10 (with 10 equal to full consciousness), a patient may be at 2 or 6 or 9, as he or she moves from deep or moderately deep coma to consciousness. The semiconscious patient may react to stimuli but not be able to speak. Next, the patient is confused, able to carry out simple commands but not clear mentally. From this stage the patient moves to full con-sciousness.

Alquinn L. Toews points out "that the patient who is unconscious is still a *person*," in spite of the inability to speak, hear, act, or react. The patient is still a child of God and should be recognized and treated as such. "When the pastor stands before an unconscious patient," the first question that must be asked, says Toews, is, "Who is this patient?"

I like to think of this in these terms: I draw a small circle and label this the "patient primary." This is the person who is lying there in bed and exhibiting most dramatically the effects of illness. Then, I like to draw a larger circle around this smaller circle and label this the "patient secondary." In this larger circle are the wife, husband, sisters, brothers, sons, daughters, parents, etc. The most effective ministry must be directed to the entire patient, both primary and secondary. This then widens the scope of ministry, for the patient is part of the social context of the family.[1]

Toews points out that this social context is an important relationship for the unconscious patient for "it helps him or her keep in touch with life's fuller context," which provides "needed resources and security."[2]

PASTORAL CARE NEEDED

Keep in mind that *hearing* is considered the last sense to be retained by the so-called unconscious patient. Therefore, the pastor should caution the family and friends that conversations about the patient should *not* be held where they may be overheard and be upsetting. While not able to respond, the patient may be aware of what is going on.

The "patient primary" may be feeling a loss of self-worth, and when family and those caring for the patient no longer speak to but only *about* the patient, that feeling can be intensified.

Toews advises that "primary support from the clergy needs to come from within through the symbols of his expression, manners, and words. . . . It is necessary that the minister come fundamentally to grips with his per-

---

1. Alquinn L. Toews, "Ministry to the Unconscious Patient," in *Pastor and Patient,* ed. Richard Dayringer (New York: Jason Aronson, 1982), p. 179.
2. Toews, p. 181.

sonal feelings and concerns so that they will not become an obstacle to his ministry, but rather through him, God's love and strength may be conveyed."[3]

Toews suggests just being present in the room with the unconscious patient, touching and speaking to the patient. A passage of Scripture or a familiar hymn may be read, and the pastor may pray aloud. Toews reminds us that many pastors who have carried out such a ministry have later been thanked by patients when they regained consciousness. Many such patients remember everything that was said around them.

Hence the precaution: *Always assume that the unconscious patient can hear!* Then your ministry can take a more aggressive role, and you and the family will avoid saying anything the patient should not hear.

Pastors also should remember the staff of the health-care team. Include them in a prayer circle around the patient; give them encouragement and affirmation for their work. This can be an indirect meaningful ministry to the patient.

PRAYER

O God, who hears us when we pray and is nearer to us than hands or feet or breathing itself, we praise and adore you. We thank you for your loving care of our lives, even when we cannot respond in word or act. We pray for *N*. We ask you to be present in a very special way in *(his/her)* life and to grant healing. Guide the doctors and other members of the health-care team. Grant them wisdom

3. Toews, p. 181.

and divine healing power. We pray for *N.*'s family members and ask you to support and encourage them as they wait and pray for *N.*'s recovery. We thank you that you have created us in your image and that we are your children. We thank you that Christ has redeemed us from the power of sin and has given us hope, faith, and love. We pray in his name. Amen.

SCRIPTURE

- Psalm 18, selected verses
- Psalm 23 (p. 171 below)
- Psalm 31, selected verses
- Psalm 107:1-9
- Romans 5:1-5 (p. 178 below)
- Romans 8:26-27 (p. 178 below)
- Romans 8:31-39 (p. 179 below)
- Philippians 4:1, 4-7 (p. 181 below)
- James 1:12 (p. 182 below)

PART III

SERVICES AND OTHER RESOURCES

21

A "SICK CALL" SERVICE OF ANOINTING

GREETING

Grace to you and peace from God Who is, Who was, and Who is to come. **Amen.**

INTRODUCTORY TEXT

We have come here to lift up before the Lord our brother/sister *Name* as we recall the words of the Apostle James who wrote: "Are any among you sick? Let them call for the elders of the church, and let the elders pray over them, anointing them with oil in the name of the Lord; and the prayers of faith will save the sick, and the Lord will raise them up; and if they have committed sins, they will be forgiven."

Reprinted from *The Book of Offices and Services After the Usage of The Order of Saint Luke,* Timothy J. Crouch, O.S.L., Editor and Compiler. Copyright 1988 by Order of Saint Luke Publications, P.O. Box 22279, Akron, Ohio 44302-0079. Used by permission.

Prayers for Healing

Let us pray:

(1) Almighty God, you are the source of all life and health: grant to all who are sick your heavenly healing, especially your child *Name* whom we lift up before you. Look upon all your faithful people who are in need and who love to call upon your Name; take them into your keeping, and deliver them from all sickness and infirmity; through Jesus Christ our Lord. **Amen.**

(or)

(2) O Living God, make us conscious now of your healing nearness. Touch our eyes that we may see you; open our ears that we may hear your voice; enter our hearts that we might know your love. Overshadow our souls and bodies with your presence, that we might partake of your strength, your love, and your healing life; in the Name of Jesus our Lord. **Amen.**

Confession and Pardon

If we say we have no sin, we deceive ourselves, and the truth is not in us. But if we confess our sins, God, who is faithful and just, will forgive our sins and cleanse us from all unrighteousness (I John 1:8-9).

Let us confess our sins before God:

**Most merciful God,
we confess that we have sinned against you
in thought, word, and deed,**

by what we have done,
and by what we have left undone.
We have not loved you with our whole heart;
we have not loved our neighbors as ourselves;
and there is no health in us.
We are truly sorry
and we humbly repent.
For the sake of our Lord Jesus Christ,
have mercy on us and forgive us,
so that we may delight in your will,
and walk in your ways,
to the glory of your holy name. Amen.

A silence is kept, followed by:

(1) Hear the Good News: "Christ died for us while we were yet sinners; that is the proof of God's love toward us."

In the Name of Jesus Christ you are forgiven. Glory to God! **Amen.**

(or)

(2) O God, absolve your people from their offenses, that through your goodness we may be delivered from those sins which in our weakness we have committed. Grant this for the sake of Jesus Christ, our blessed Lord and Savior. **Amen.**

(THANKSGIVING OVER THE OIL)

O God, the giver of health and salvation, we give thanks to you for the gift of oil that, as your holy apostles anointed many who were sick and healed them, your Holy

Spirit may come upon us and on this gift so that those who in faith and repentance receive this anointing may be made whole; through the Name of Jesus Christ our Lord we pray. **Amen.**

ANOINTING (LAYING ON OF HANDS)

Name I anoint you with oil (lay hands upon you) in the name of the Father, and of the Son, and of the Holy Spirit. **Amen.**

PRAYER AFTER ANOINTING (LAYING ON OF HANDS)

Almighty God, you are ever more ready to hear than we are to pray, and to give more than we either desire or deserve: We give you thanks for listening to our prayers for our sick *brother(s)/sister(s)*. As your will directs, we have confidence that you will deliver *him/her/them* from evil, preserve *him/her/them* in all goodness, and bring *Name/them* to everlasting life; through Jesus Christ our Lord. **Amen.**

THE GREAT THANKSGIVING

Lift up your heart*(s)* and give thanks to the Lord our God.

Almighty God, Creator of heaven and earth, you made us in your image, to love and be loved. When we turned away, and our love failed, your love remained steadfast. By the suffering, death, and resurrection of your only Son Jesus Christ you delivered us from slavery to sin and death and made us a new covenant by water and the Spirit.

On the night he gave himself up for us he took bread,

gave thanks to you, broke the bread, gave it to his disciples, and said: "Take, eat; this is my body which is given for you. Do this in remembrance of me."

When the supper was over he took the cup, gave it to his disciples, and said: "Drink from this, all of you; for this is my blood of the new covenant, poured out for you and for many for the forgiveness of sins. Do this, as often as you drink it, in remembrance of me."

And so, in remembrance of these your mighty acts in Jesus Christ, we offer ourselves in praise and thanksgiving, as a holy and living sacrifice, in union with Christ's offering for us.

Pour out your Holy Spirit on us and on these gifts of bread and wine. Make them be for us the Body and Blood of Christ, that we may be for the world the Body of Christ, redeemed by his Blood.

By your Spirit make us one with Christ, one with one another, and one in ministry to all the world, until Christ comes in final victory and we feast at his heavenly banquet. Through your Son Jesus Christ, with the Holy Spirit in your holy Church, all honor and glory is yours, Almighty God, now and for ever. **Amen.**

And now with the confidence of children of God, let us pray:

Our Father in heaven, hallowed be your name.
Your kingdom come, your will be done
on earth as in heaven.
Give us this day our daily bread.
Forgive us our sins
as we forgive those who sin against us.

Save us from the time of trial,
and deliver us from evil.
For the kingdom, the power and the glory are yours,
now and for ever. Amen.

(or the traditional language may be used)

GIVING THE BREAD AND CUP

The sacrament is exchanged with these words:

The Body of Christ, given for you. **Amen.**
The Blood of Christ, given for you. **Amen.**

PRAYER AFTER COMMUNION (POSTCOMMUNION)

Eternal God, we give you thanks for this holy mystery in which you have given yourself to us. Grant that it might strengthen our faith, redeem our weakness and bring us to everlasting salvation. We praise you, Blessed and Holy Trinity, One God, now and for ever. **Amen.**

DISMISSAL WITH BLESSING

The Almighty God, who is a strong tower to all who put their trust therein, to whom all things in heaven and on earth, and under the earth, bow and obey: Be now and always your defense, and make you know and feel that the only Name under heaven given for health and salvation is the Name of our Lord Jesus Christ.

The blessing of God Almighty preserve you in peace. **Amen.**

22

THE BAPTISMAL COVENANT

[Sections having to do with confirmation, reaffirmation of faith, and reception into the church have been omitted. Some modification of the service for use with the sick has been made. Pastors will want to further shape the service to the particular situation.]

INTRODUCTION TO THE SERVICE

Brother(s) and sister(s) in Christ:

Through the Sacrament of Baptism, believers and their households are initiated into Christ's holy Church. We are incorporated into God's mighty acts of salvation and given new birth through water and the Spirit. All this is God's gift, offered to us without price.

RENUNCIATION OF SIN AND PROFESSION OF FAITH

[Circumstances will determine how much of the following should be used.] The minister addresses parents or other sponsors and those candidates who can answer for themselves:

From *The Book of Services.* Copyright © 1985 by The United Methodist Publishing House. Used by permission.

On behalf of the whole church, I ask you:
Do you reject the spiritual forces of wickedness,
the evil powers of this world,
and the bondage of sin?
I do.

Do you accept the freedom and power God gives you to resist evil, injustice, and oppression in whatever forms they present themselves?
I do.

Do you confess Jesus Christ as your Savior,
put your whole trust in his grace,
and promise to serve him as your Lord,
in union with the Church which Christ has opened to
people of all ages, nations, and races?
I do.

[The following is used when appropriate.]
The minister addresses parents or other sponsors of candidates not able to answer for themselves:

Will you nurture *these (children/persons)*
in Christ's holy Church,
that by your teaching and example *(they)* may be
guided to respond to God's grace,
openly to profess their faith,
and to lead a Christian life?
I will.

The minister addresses candidates who can answer for themselves (and their sponsors):

According to the grace given to you,
will you remain *faithful members* of Christ's holy Church
and serve as Christ's *representatives* in the world?
[And will you who sponsor *these candidates* support and
encourage *them* in their Christian life?]
I will.

[When appropriate, the following may be addressed to members of the congregation present:]

Will you nurture one another in the Christian faith and
life and include *these persons* now before you in your care?
[A response of "We will" may be given.]

*[The minister may ask the candidate for baptism to affirm
(his/her) faith by responding "I do" to the following questions:]*

Do you believe in God the Father?
Do you believe in Jesus Christ?
Do you believe in the Holy Spirit?

*[Or the Apostles' Creed may be affirmed by candidates and
congregation:]*

I believe in God, the Father Almighty,
Creator of heaven and earth.
I believe in Jesus Christ, his only Son, our Lord.
He was conceived by the power of the Holy Spirit
and was born of the Virgin Mary.
He suffered under Pontius Pilate,
was crucified, died, and was buried.

He descended to the dead.
On the third day he rose again.
He ascended into heaven,
and is seated at the right hand of the Father.
He will come again
to judge the living and the dead.
I believe in the Holy Spirit,
the holy catholic Church,
the communion of saints,
the forgiveness of sins,
the resurrection of the body,
and the life everlasting. **Amen.**

Thanksgiving over the Water

*[Discretion may be used in selecting part or all of the fol-
lowing.]*
Water may be poured into the font at this time.
*[A family member or nurse may assist, holding a container
of water.]*

The Lord be with you.
And also with you.

Let us pray.
Eternal Father:
When nothing existed but chaos
you swept across the dark waters
and brought forth light.
In the days of Noah
you saved those on the ark through water.
After the Flood you set in the clouds a rainbow.

When you saw your people as slaves in Egypt,
you led them to freedom through the sea.
Their children you brought through the Jordan
to the land which you promised. . . .
Pour out your Holy Spirit,
to bless this gift of water
and those who receive it,
to wash away their sin
and clothe them in righteousness
throughout their lives,
that, dying and being raised with Christ,
they may share in his final victory.
Amen.

BAPTISM WITH LAYING ON OF HANDS

As each candidate is baptized, the minister says:

N, I baptize you in the name of the Father,
and of the Son,
and of the Holy Spirit. **Amen.**

*Immediately after the administration of the water, as hands
are placed on the head of each person by the minister and
by others if desired, the minister says to each:*

The Holy Spirit work within you,
that being born through water and the Spirit,
you may be a faithful disciple of Jesus Christ.
Amen.

The minister addresses those newly received:

The God of all grace,
who has called us to eternal glory in Christ,
establish and strengthen you
by the power of the Holy Spirit,
that you may live in grace and peace.

*One or more lay members may join with the minister in acts
and words of welcome and peace.*

*Appropriate thanksgivings and intercessions for those who
have participated in these acts should be included in the
concerns and prayers that follow.*

23

THE LORD'S SUPPER
(MINIMUM TEXT)

The people come together
and exchange greetings in the Lord's name.
Scriptures are read and interpreted.
Prayer and praise are offered.

The minister then gives this or some other suitable invitation:
    Christ our Lord invites to his table all who love him
and seek to grow into his likeness. Let us draw near with
faith, make our humble confession, and prepare to receive
this holy Sacrament.

Minister and People: **We do not presume to come to this
your table, merciful Lord, trusting in our own goodness,
but in your unfailing mercies. We are not worthy that you
should receive us, but give your word and we shall be
healed, through Jesus Christ our Lord. Amen.**

The minister may say: Hear the good news: "Christ died
for us while we were yet sinners; that is proof of God's

---

love toward us." In the name of Jesus Christ, you are forgiven!

All may exchange signs and words of God's peace.

The minister takes the bread and cup, prepares the bread and wine for the meal, and then prays the Great Thanksgiving as follows:
Lift up your heart(s) and give thanks to the Lord our God.

Father Almighty, Creator of heaven and earth, you made us in your image, to love and to be loved. When we turned away, and our love failed, your love remained steadfast. By the suffering, death, and resurrection of your only Son Jesus Christ you delivered us from slavery to sin and death and made with us a new covenant by water and the Spirit.

On the night in which he gave himself up for us he took bread, gave thanks to you, broke the bread, gave it to his disciples, and said, "Take, eat; this is my body which is given for you. Do this in remembrance of me."

When the supper was over he took the cup, gave thanks to you, gave it to his disciples, and said, "Drink from this, all of you; for this is my blood of the new covenant, poured out for you and for many for the forgiveness of sins. Do this, as often as you drink it, in remembrance of me."

And so, in remembrance of these your mighty acts in Jesus Christ, we offer ourselves in praise and thanksgiving as a holy and living sacrifice, in union with Christ's offering for us.

Pour out your Holy Spirit on us and on these gifts of bread and wine. Make them be for us the body and blood of Christ, that we may be for the world the body of Christ, redeemed by his blood.

By your Spirit make us one with Christ, one with each other, and one in ministry to all the world, until Christ comes in final victory, and we feast at his heavenly banquet.

Through your Son Jesus Christ, with the Holy Spirit in your holy Church, all honor and glory is yours, Almighty Father, now and for ever. Amen.

And now, with the confidence of children of God, let us pray:

Our Father in heaven,
hallowed be your Name,
your kingdom come,
your will be done, on earth as in heaven.
Give us today our daily bread.
Forgive us our sins
as we forgive those who sin against us.
Save us from the time of trial,
and deliver us from evil.
For the kingdom, the power, and the glory are yours,
now and for ever. Amen.

The minister breaks the bread.
The bread and wine are given to the people,
with these or other words being exchanged:

The body of Christ, given for you. **Amen.**

The blood of Christ, given for you. **Amen.**

When all have received, the Lord's table is put in order.
The minister may then give thanks after Communion.
A final hymn or song may be sung.

The minister gives this final blessing:
    The grace of the Lord Jesus Christ, and the love of God, and the communion of the Holy Spirit be with you all. **Amen.**

24

PRAYERS, POEMS, HYMNS

The Serenity Prayer

God, give us grace to accept with serenity the things
that cannot be changed, courage to change the things
which should be changed, and the wisdom to
distinguish the one from the other.

— Reinhold Niebuhr

The Confederate Soldier's Prayer

I asked God for strength, that I might achieve;
I was made weak, that I might learn humbly to obey.
I asked for help, that I might do greater things;
I was given infirmity, that I might do better things.
I asked for riches, that I might be happy;
I was given poverty, that I might be wise.
I asked for power, that I might have the praise of men;
I was given weakness, that I might feel the need of God.
I asked for all things, that I might enjoy my life;

I was given life, that I might enjoy all things.
I received nothing I asked for, but everything I had
   hoped for.
I am among men, most richly blessed.

— Anonymous

Poems and Hymns

God Hath Not Promised

Blessed be the LORD who has given rest to his people Israel, according to all that he promised; not one word has failed of all his good promise, which he uttered by Moses his servant.
— 1 Kings 8:56, RSV

God hath not promised skies always blue,
   Flower-strewn pathways all our lives through.
God hath not promised sun without rain,
   Joy without sorrow, peace without pain.
But God hath promised strength for the day,
   Rest for the laborer, light on the way,
Grace for the trial, help from above,
   Unfailing sympathy, undying love.
— Annie Flint Johnson

What a Friend We Have in Jesus

What a friend we have in Jesus,
All our sins and griefs to bear!
What a privilege to carry
Everything to God in prayer!

O what peace we often forfeit,
O what needless pain we bear,
All because we do not carry
Everything to God in prayer!

Have we trials and temptations?
Is there trouble anywhere?
We should never be discouraged;
Take it to the Lord in prayer!
Can we find a friend so faithful
Who will all our sorrows share?
Jesus knows our every weakness;
Take it to the Lord in prayer.

Are we weak and heavy laden,
Cumbered with a load of care?
Precious Savior, still our refuge:
Take it to the Lord in prayer.
Do thy friends despise, forsake thee?
Take it to the Lord in prayer!
In his arms he'll take and shield thee;
Thou wilt find a solace there.

— Joseph M. Scriven

There Is a Place of Quiet Rest

There is a place of quiet rest,
Near to the heart of God,
A place where sin cannot molest,
Near to the heart of God.

Refrain:
O Jesus, blest Redeemer,
Sent from the heart of God,
Hold us who wait before Thee,
Near to the heart of God.

There is a place of comfort sweet,
Near to the heart of God,
A place where we our Savior meet,
Near to the heart of God.
Refrain

There is a place of full release,
Near to the heart of God,
A place where all is joy and peace,
Near to the heart of God.
Refrain

— Cleland B. McAfee

Now Thank We All Our God

Now thank we all our God
   with heart and hands and voices,
who wondrous things hath done,
   in whom this world rejoices;
who, from our mothers' arms
   hath bless'd us on our way
with countless gifts of love,
   and still is ours today.

O may this bounteous God
   through all our life be near us,
with ever joyful hearts

and blessed peace to cheer us;
and keep us in his grace,
    and guide us when perplexed,
and free us from all ills
    in this world and the next.

All praise and thanks to God
    the Father now be given,
the Son, and him who reigns
    with them in highest heaven,
the one eternal God,
    Whom heav'n and earth adore;
for thus it was, is now,
    and shall be evermore.

— Martin Rinckart

25

SELECTED SCRIPTURE PASSAGES

OLD TESTAMENT

Numbers 6:24-26
The LORD bless you and keep you;
the LORD make his face to shine upon you, and be
   gracious to you;
the LORD lift up his countenance upon you, and give
   you peace.

Deuteronomy 33:27
The eternal God is your dwelling place,
and underneath are the everlasting arms. *(RSV)*

Psalm 23
The LORD is my shepherd, I shall not want.
   He makes me lie down in green pastures;
he leads me beside still waters;
   he restores my soul.
He leads me in right paths
   for his name's sake.

Even though I walk through the darkest valley,
   I fear no evil;
for you are with me;

your rod and your staff —
   they comfort me.

You prepare a table before me
   in the presence of my enemies;
you anoint my head with oil;
   my cup overflows.
Surely goodness and mercy shall follow me
   all the days of my life,
and I shall dwell in the house of the LORD
   my whole life long.

Psalm 100

Make a joyful noise to the LORD, all the earth.
   Worship the LORD with gladness;
   come into his presence with singing.

Know that the LORD is God.
   It is he that made us, and we are his;
   we are his people, and the sheep of his pasture.

Enter his gates with thanksgiving,
   and his courts with praise.
   Give thanks to him, bless his name.

For the LORD is good;
   his steadfast love endures forever,
   and his faithfulness to all generations.

Psalm 121

I lift up my eyes to the hills —
   from where will my help come?
My help comes from the LORD,
   who made heaven and earth.

He will not let your foot be moved;
   he who keeps you will not slumber.
He who keeps Israel
   will neither slumber nor sleep.

The LORD is your keeper;
   the LORD is your shade at your right hand.
The sun shall not strike you by day,
   nor the moon by night.

The LORD will keep you from all evil;
   he will keep your life.
The LORD will keep
   your going out and your coming in
   from this time on and forevermore.

Proverbs 17:22

A cheerful heart is a good medicine,
   but a downcast spirit dries up the bones. *(NRSV)*

Being cheerful keeps you healthy. It is slow death to be gloomy all the time. *(Good News Bible)*

Isaiah 40:28-31

Have you not known? Have you not heard?
The LORD is the everlasting God,
   the Creator of the ends of the earth.
He does not faint or grow weary;
   his understanding is unsearchable.
He gives power to the faint,
   and strengthens the powerless.
Even youths will faint and be weary,

and the young will fall exhausted;
but those who wait for the LORD shall renew
    their strength,
  they shall mount up with wings like eagles,
they shall run and not be weary,
  they shall walk and not faint.

Isaiah 55:10-13

For as the rain and the snow come down from heaven,
  and do not return there until they have watered
    the earth,
making it bring forth and sprout,
  giving seed to the sower and bread to the eater,
so shall my word be that goes out from my mouth;
  it shall not return to me empty,
but it shall accomplish that which I purpose,
  and succeed in the thing for which I sent it.

For you shall go out in joy,
  and be led back in peace;
the mountains and the hills before you
  shall burst into song,
  and all the trees of the field shall clap their hands.
Instead of the thorn shall come up the cypress;
  instead of the brier shall come up the myrtle;
and it shall be to the LORD for a memorial,
  for an everlasting sign that shall not be cut off.

Jeremiah 17:7-8, 14

Blessed are those who trust in the LORD,
  whose trust is the LORD.

They shall be like a tree planted by water,
    sending out its roots by the stream.
It shall not fear when heat comes,
    and its leaves shall stay green;
in the year of drought it is not anxious,
    and it does not cease to bear fruit. . . .

Heal me, O LORD, and I shall be healed;
    save me, and I shall be saved;
    for you are my praise.

Lamentations 3:55-58
I called on your name, O LORD,
    from the depths of the pit;
you heard my plea, "Do not close your ear
    to my cry for help, but give me relief!"
You came near when I called on you;
    you said, "Do not fear!"

You have taken up my cause, O LORD,
    you have redeemed my life.

New Testament

Matthew 9:27-33
As Jesus went on from there, two blind men followed him,
crying aloud, "Have mercy on us, Son of David!" When
he entered the house, the blind men came to him; and
Jesus said to them, "Do you believe that I am able to do
this?" They said to him, "Yes, Lord." Then he touched their
eyes and said, "According to your faith let it be done to

you." And their eyes were opened. Then Jesus sternly ordered them, "See that no one knows of this." But they went away and spread the news about him throughout that district.

After they had gone away, a demoniac who was mute was brought to him. And when the demon had been cast out, the one who had been mute spoke; and the crowds were amazed and said, "Never has anything like this been seen in Israel."

Matthew 11:28-30

"Come to me, all you that are weary and are carrying heavy burdens, and I will give you rest. Take my yoke upon you, and learn from me; for I am gentle and humble in heart, and you will find rest for your souls. For my yoke is easy, and my burden is light."

Mark 2:1-5, 11-12

When he returned to Capernaum after some days, it was reported that he was at home. So many gathered around that there was no longer room for them, not even in front of the door; and he was speaking the word to them. Then some people came, bringing to him a paralyzed man, carried by four of them. And when they could not bring him to Jesus because of the crowd, they removed the roof above him; and after having dug through it, they let down the mat on which the paralytic lay. When Jesus saw their faith, he said to the paralytic, "Son, your sins are forgiven." . . . "I say to you, stand up, take your mat and go to your home." And he stood up, and immediately took the mat and went out before all of them;

so that they were all amazed and glorified God, saying, "We have never seen anything like this!"

Luke 11:9-10

"So I say to you, Ask, and it will be given you; search, and you will find; knock, and the door will be opened for you. For everyone who asks receives, and everyone who searches finds, and for everyone who knocks, the door will be opened."

Luke 18:15-17

People were bringing even infants to him that he might touch them; and when the disciples saw it, they sternly ordered them not to do it. But Jesus called for them and said, "Let the little children come to me, and do not stop them; for it is to such as these that the kingdom of God belongs. Truly, I tell you, whoever does not receive the kingdom of God as a little child will never enter it."

John 3:16-18

"For God so loved the world that he gave his only Son, so that everyone who believes in him may not perish but may have eternal life.

"Indeed, God did not send the Son into the world to condemn the world, but in order that the world might be saved through him. Those who believe in him are not condemned; but those who do not believe are condemned already, because they have not believed in the name of the only Son of God."

John 14:1-7

"Do not let your hearts be troubled. Believe in God, believe also in me. In my Father's house there are many dwelling places. If it were not so, would I have told you that I go to prepare a place for you? And if I go and prepare a place for you, I will come again and will take you to myself, so that where I am, there you may be also. And you know the way to the place I am going." Thomas said to him, "Lord, we do not know where you are going. How can we know the way?" Jesus said to him, "I am the way, and the truth, and the life. No one comes to the Father except through me. If you know me, you will know my Father also. From now on you do know him and have seen him."

Romans 5:1 5

Therefore, since we are justified by faith, we have peace with God through our Lord Jesus Christ, through whom we have obtained access to this grace in which we stand; and we boast in our hope of sharing the glory of God. And not only that, but we also boast in our sufferings, knowing that suffering produces endurance, and endurance produces character, and character produces hope, and hope does not disappoint us, because God's love has been poured into our hearts through the Holy Spirit that has been given to us.

Romans 8:26-27

Likewise the Spirit helps us in our weakness; for we do not know how to pray as we ought, but that very Spirit intercedes with sighs too deep for words. And God, who searches the heart, knows what is the mind of the Spirit, because the Spirit intercedes for the saints according to the will of God.

Romans 8:28-30

We know that all things work together for good for those who love God, who are called according to his purpose. For those whom he foreknew he also predestined to be conformed to the image of his Son, in order that he might be the firstborn within a large family. And those whom he predestined he also called; and those whom he called he also justified; and those whom he justified he also glorified.

Romans 8:31-39

What then are we to say about these things? If God is for us, who is against us? He who did not withhold his own Son, but gave him up for all of us, will he not with him also give us everything else? Who will bring any charge against God's elect? It is God who justifies. Who is to condemn? It is Christ Jesus, who died, yes, who was raised, who is at the right hand of God, who indeed intercedes for us. Who will separate us from the love of Christ? Will hardship, or distress, or persecution, or famine, or nakedness, or peril, or sword? As it is written,

> "For your sake we are being killed all day long;
>   we are accounted as sheep to be slaughtered."

No, in all these things we are more than conquerors through him who loved us. For I am convinced that neither death, nor life, nor angels, nor rulers, nor things present, nor things to come, nor powers, nor height, nor depth, nor anything else in all creation, will be able to separate us from the love of God in Christ Jesus our Lord.

Romans 10:8*b*-13

> "The word is near you, on your lips and in your heart"

(that is, the word of faith that we proclaim); because if you confess with your lips that Jesus is Lord and believe in your heart that God raised him from the dead, you will be saved. For one believes with the heart and so is justified, and one confesses with the mouth and so is saved. The scripture says, "No one who believes in him will be put to shame." For there is no distinction between Jew and Greek; the same Lord is Lord of all and is generous to all who call on him. For, "Everyone who calls on the name of the Lord shall be saved."

2 Corinthians 4:7-9, 16-18

But we have this treasure in clay jars, so that it may be made clear that this extraordinary power belongs to God and does not come from us. We are afflicted in every way, but not crushed; perplexed, but not driven to despair; persecuted, but not forsaken; struck down, but not destroyed. . . .

So we do not lose heart. Even though our outer nature is wasting away, our inner nature is being renewed day by day. For this slight momentary affliction is preparing us for an eternal weight of glory beyond all measure, because we look not at what can be seen but at what cannot be seen; for what can be seen is temporary, but what cannot be seen is eternal.

Philippians 4:1, 4-7

Therefore, my brothers and sisters, whom I love and long for, my joy and crown, stand firm in the Lord in this way, my beloved. . . .

Rejoice in the Lord always; again I will say, Rejoice. Let your gentleness be known to everyone. The Lord is near. Do not worry about anything, but in everything by prayer and supplication with thanksgiving let your requests be made known to God. And the peace of God, which surpasses all understanding, will guard your hearts and your minds in Christ Jesus.

Philippians 4:8

Finally, beloved, whatever is true, whatever is honorable, whatever is just, whatever is pure, whatever is pleasing, whatever is commendable, if there is any excellence and if there is anything worthy of praise, think about these things.

Philippians 4:10-13, 19

I rejoice in the Lord greatly that now at last you have revived your concern for me; indeed, you were concerned for me, but had no opportunity to show it. Not that I am referring to being in need; for I have learned to be content with whatever I have. I know what it is to have little, and I know what it is to have plenty. In any and all circumstances I have learned the secret of being well-fed and of going hungry, of having plenty and of being in need. I can do all things through him who strengthens me. . . .

. . . And my God will fully satisfy every need of yours according to his riches in glory in Christ Jesus.

Hebrews 11:1-3, 8-12

Now faith is the assurance of things hoped for, the conviction of things not seen. Indeed, by faith our ancestors received approval. By faith we understand that the worlds were prepared by the word of God, so that what is seen was made from things that are not visible. . . .

By faith Abraham obeyed when he was called to set out for a place that he was to receive as an inheritance; and he set out, not knowing where he was going. By faith he stayed for a time in the land he had been promised, as in a foreign land, living in tents, as did Isaac and Jacob, who were heirs with him of the same promise. For he looked forward to the city that has foundations, whose architect and builder is God. By faith he received power of procreation, even though he was too old — and Sarah herself was barren — because he considered him faithful who had promised. Therefore from one person, and this one as good as dead, descendants were born, "as many as the stars of heaven and as the innumerable grains of sand by the seashore."

James 1:12

Blessed is anyone who endures temptation. Such a one has stood the test and will receive the crown of life that the Lord has promised to those who love him.

Revelation 21:1-5

Then I saw a new heaven and a new earth; for the first heaven and the first earth had passed away, and the sea was no more. And I saw the holy city, the new Jerusalem, coming down out of heaven from God, prepared as a bride adorned for her husband. And I heard a loud voice from the throne saying,

"See, the home of God is among mortals.
He will dwell with them as their God;
they will be his peoples,
and God himself will be with them;
he will wipe every tear from their eyes.
Death will be no more;
mourning and crying and pain will be no more,
for the first things have passed away."

And the one who was seated on the throne said, "See, I am making all things new."

BIBLIOGRAPHY

Books

Alvarez, A. *The Savage God: A Study of Suicide.* New York: Random House, 1972.

Becker, Arthur H. *The Compassionate Visitor.* Minneapolis: Augsburg Publishing House, 1985.

Becker, Ernest. *The Denial of Death.* New York: The Free Press, 1973.

Biddle, Perry H., Jr. *Humor and Healing.* Ft. Lauderdale, FL: Desert Ministries, Inc. (P.O. Box 2001, Zip: 33303), 1994.

—————. *Reflections on Suicide.* Ft. Lauderdale, FL: Desert Ministries, Inc. (P.O. Box 2001, Zip: 33303), 1992.

Biegert, John E. *Looking Up . . . While Lying Down.* New York: The Pilgrim Press, 1978. Inspirational booklet to give patients. Widely used and highly recommended.

Calhoun, Gerald J. *Pastoral Companionship.* New York: Paulist Press, 1986. Guidance for ministry with the seriously ill and their families.

Catherall, Don R. *Back from the Brink.* New York: Bantam Books, 1992. An outstanding tool for understanding trauma victims and helping them and their families.

Cousins, Norman. *Head First, the Biology of Hope.* New York: E. P. Dutton, 1989.

Dayringer, Richard, ed. *Pastor and Patient.* New York: Jason Aronson, 1982.

Dobihal, Edward F., Jr., and Charles W. Stewart. *When a Friend Is Dying: A Guide to Caring for the Terminally Ill and Bereaved.* Nashville: Abingdon Press, 1984.

Dorland's Pocket Medical Dictionary. Philadelphia: W. B. Saunders Co., 1968.

Doyle, Paul Barton, and John Ishee. *In Step with God.* Brentwood, TN: New Directions (a division of JM Productions, P.O. Box 1911, Brentwood, TN 37024-1911), 1993. Useful for persons with addictions.

————. *Spirituality in Recovery: A Twelve Step Approach.* Brentwood, TN: New Directions (a division of JM Productions, P.O. Box 1911, Brentwood, TN 37024-1911), 1993. Can be used with persons with addictions of any kind.

Greenstone, James L., and Sharon C. Leviton. *Elements of Crisis Intervention.* Pacific Grove, CA: Brooks/Cole, 1993.

Hauerwas, Stanley. *Naming the Silences: God, Medicine, and the Problem of Suffering.* Grand Rapids: William B. Eerdmans, 1990. An excellent resource for better understanding suffering and supporting those who suffer.

Haugk, Kenneth C. *Christian Caregiving.* Minneapolis: Augsburg Publishing House, 1984.

Hesch, John B. *Clinical Pastoral Care for Hospitalized Children and Their Families.* New York: Paulist Press, 1987.

Holst, Lawrence E., ed. *Hospital Ministry.* New York: Crossroad, 1985.

Irion, Paul E. *Hospice and Ministry.* Nashville: Abingdon Press, 1988.

Janoff-Bulman, Ronnie. *Shattered Assumptions: Towards a*

New Psychology of Trauma. New York: The Free Press/Macmillan, 1992.

Klein, Allen. *The Healing Power of Humor.* Los Angeles: Jeremy P. Tarcher, Inc., 1989. Shows you how to laugh and what it can do for you.

Lederer, Richard. *Get Thee to a Punnery.* New York: Dell Publishing, 1988. One of several humorous books by the same author to use with or give to patients.

Lester, Andrew D., ed. *When Children Suffer.* Philadelphia: Westminster Press, 1987.

Martin, Francis. *Prayers for Recovery.* Brentwood, TN: New Directions (a division of JM Productions, P.O. Box 1911, Brentwood, TN 37024-1911), 1993. Inspirational prayers for persons recovering from addictions.

McFarland, John Robert. *Now That I Have Cancer I Am Whole.* Kansas City: Andrews and McMeel, 1993.

Murphy, Miriam. *Prayer in Action.* Nashville: Abingdon, 1979. Can be a useful tool for patients in learning to pray for their recovery.

Ohsberg, H. Oliver. *The Church and Persons with Handicaps.* Scottsdale, PA: Herald Press, 1982.

Peale, Norman Vincent. *Positive Imaging.* Pawling, NY: The Foundation for Christian Living, 1982.

Peckham, Charles, and Arline B. Peckham. *I Can Still Pray.* Lebanon, OH: Otterbein Home, 1979. Help for those visiting in nursing homes.

————. *Thank You for Shaking My Hand.* Lebanon, OH: Otterbein Home, 1986. A guidebook for training volunteer visitors in nursing homes.

Peter, Lawrence J., and Bill Dana. *The Laughter Prescription.* New York: Ballantine Books, 1982. A guide to achieving health and happiness through humor.

Reimer, Lawrence D., and James T. Wagner. *The Hospital Handbook*. Wilton, CT: Morehouse Barlow, 1984.

Robinson, Vera M. *Humor and the Health Professions*. Thorofare, NJ: Slack Incorporate, 1991.

Rosten, Leo. *Leo Rosten's Giant Book of Laughter*. New York: Bonanza, 1985. A fresh and classy collection of jokes and humor to use with patients.

Samara, Cal. *The Joyful Christ: The Healing Powers of Humor*. San Francisco: Harper & Row, 1986. This book will help pastors use the healing power of joy and humor in visiting the sick.

Siegel, Bernie S. *Love, Medicine and Miracles*. New York: Harper & Row, 1986.

———. *Peace, Love and Healing: Bodymind Communication*. New York: Harper & Row, 1989.

Styron, William. *Darkness Visible*. New York: Random House, 1990. A memoir of madness and near suicide by a noted novelist.

Taber's Cyclopedic Medical Dictionary. Philadelphia: F. A. Davis, 1981.

Trueblood, Elton. *The Humor of Christ*. New York: Harper/Collins Publishers, 1964. A classic on the subject.

Twelve Steps and Twelve Traditions. New York: Alcoholics Anonymous World Services, 1986.

Worden, J. William. *Grief Counseling and Grief Therapy*. New York: Springer Publishing Co., 1982.

Zaner, Richard M. *Troubled Voices: Stories of Ethics and Illness*. Cleveland: The Pilgrim Press, 1993. An outstanding new book to help pastors and others involved in clinical ethical decisions by one of America's leading clinical ethicists.

Other Resources

"Christian Ministry," 407 S. Dearborn St., Chicago, IL 60605. Write for special issues and articles dealing with illness and pastoral care.

"Joyful Noiseletter," published by Fellowship of Merry Christians, P.O. Box 895, Portage, MI 49081-0895. Contains cartoons and funny stories, etc., that can be used in church newsletters and with patients.

"Journal of Pastoral Care," P.O. Box 326, Rt. 222 and Sharadin Rd., Kutztown, PA 19530.

"Laughing Matters," published by The Humor Project, Inc., 110 Springs St., Saratoga Springs, NY 12866. Dr. Joel Goodman is the publisher; he directs an annual weekend humor conference which relates humor to health issues, business, and education.

"Pastoral Psychology," Subscription Dept., Human Sciences Press, Inc., 233 Spring St., New York, NY 10013-1578.

Video stores rent classical comedy films. Record shops sell audiotapes of well-known comedians which can be given or loaned to patients.

Bookstores stock paperback books by popular humorous writers. A church might develop its own "Humor Cart" of books, tapes, videos, gags, balloons, etc., to loan or give patients in the hospital or recovering at home. Videos of the popular TV series *M*A*S*H*, especially the last two episodes in the series, give insights into the use of humor in the hospital setting.

Regional conferences on humor and healing are being conducted. Church members might be sent to a local conference or to The Humor Project, Inc., annual conference (see above). An intentional use of humor can make a difference in the attitude and healing of patients and make life easier for family, friends, and health-care workers.